THE ROBUST ORGANIZATION

ORGANIZATION

Transforming Your Company
Using Adaptive Design

THE ROBUST ORGANIZATION

Transforming Your Company Using Adaptive Design

WILLIAM A. STIMSON

IRWIN
Professional Publishing®
Chicago • London • Singapore

Times Mirror
Higher Education Group

Library of Congress Cataloging-in-Publication Data

Stimson, William A.
    The robust organization : transforming your company using adaptive
    design / William A. Stimson.
        p.   cm.
    Includes index.
    ISBN 0–7863–0859–1
    1. Corporate reorganizations—United States—Management.
    2. Reengineering (Management)—United States.   3. Industrial
    management—United States.   4. Entrepreneurship—United States.
    I. Title.
    HD2746.55.U5S75   1996
    658.4'063—dc20   96–3562

Printed in the United States of America
1 2 3 4 5 6 7 8 9 0 BS 3 2 1 0 9 8 7 6

To my wife Josette Henriette Louise,
who bandages my wounds and keeps me going.
Fille de Saintonge,
je t'aime, je t'aimerai toujours.

FOREWORD

This is an unusual book by an unusual individual.

Anyone who has met and interacted with William Stimson in a classroom setting knows something about his determined pursuit of knowledge and his keen sense of practicality. After reading this book they will also have some appreciation for the intellectual breadth of the man and for his ability to clarify difficult subjects. There is something in these pages for anyone interested in the management of change, in organizations big or small. There is also something for virtually anyone who simply wants to know more about some of the concepts and tools which apply to organization and process dynamics. It is a book which will be referred to repeatedly for the wealth of information, knowledge, and insight between its covers.

Edward W. Davis
The Oliver Wight Professor
The Darden Graduate School of Business
University of Virginia

PREFACE

In his 1970 book *Future Shock*, Alvin Toffler talked about the acceleration of human development. As an example, he said that everything from goods and services to scientific publications is doubling every 15 years, and that this doubling period is decreasing. Toffler pointed out that only a few generations ago, the world one departed was much like the world into which one was born. But today, the world is vastly different from the world of 60 years ago, and this difference will increase, threatening the ability of the human mind to adjust to the rate of change in a single life span. Two popular sellers of recent years reinforce this notion. James Gleick's *Chaos: Making a New Science* and Tom Peters' *Thriving on Chaos*, both serious works in the fields of science and business, respectively, describe a world that is approaching the steep part of an exponential curve of change.

Certainly, change is upon us, culturally, technologically, and economically. In the postwar period, Japan and Western Europe have gradually overcome the annihilation of their industrial capacity, which left the United States for so many years the unchallenged leader in the production of goods and services. Today their competition is fierce, accelerating yet again the technological developments that Toffler talked about. A glance at the current business literature echoes the theme: a company must change, and change radically, in order to survive. We hear that companies must undergo "reengineering," "total transformation," "strategic change," even "disorganization," in order to keep up.

Keep up to what? The competition, of course, but if we are talking about goods and services, the timeless factor is quality. A lack of concern for quality is, arbitrarily, the Achilles heel that we exposed to our competitors. Unchallenged during nearly two generations, American manufacturers let quality slide. The abandonment of product quality in American industry following World War II has been so well documented that we will assume it as fact and only mention in passing the term *planned obsolescence* of American products from the fifties through the seventies.

The challenge of postwar Japan, in particular, brought us to our senses. We began to realize that our economy was global. Americans would and did purchase foreign products if they believed that those products had superior quality. Strategies such as import quotas and appeals to patriotism didn't seem to work. When all else failed, American industry understood the message and began a return to manufacturing quality products. Many companies are getting on board as the realization becomes overpowering: With NAFTA, GATT, and the world market, you can sell your products if they are cheap or good or both. Otherwise, you're out of business.

It is one thing for the CEO of a company to give the order: "We gotta reengineer!" It is something else to bring about the needed changes effectively, systematically, and robustly. At a given moment, capital, resources, and skill must all come together. And if you want to do it twice (or more), you better have organization. This book is about how to organize your company and your processes so that you can do something over and over again, better and better, maybe even in the face of chaos.

Years ago, Charles Atlas used to run an advertisement in men's magazines that was titled "The 97-Pound Weakling." In the form of a comic strip, it showed a skinny fellow on the beach being pushed around by a bully, who then made off with the victim's girlfriend. The weakling would go home, read his magazine, then declare "Darn it! I'm tired of being pushed around. I'm sending off for this Charles Atlas dynamic tension program!"

In today's business environment, you don't have to be a 97-pound weakling in order to be beset by bullies. You can run a respected product or service, but the competition is fierce and global, and the ammunition is quality. This book will show you how to get the competitive bullies off your back and keep your customers. The way to consistent high quality, irrespective of market and process dynamics, is by organizing your company to robust structure. A robust organization starts from the beginning—the *real* beginning. Where do you want to go? What's the best way to get there? You exploit all the talent in your company to determine answers to some very fundamental questions concerning mission, goals, and methods.

Then you design, build, and conduct your processes so that they constantly maintain target no matter what the disturbances, and even when the target changes, as it must if improvement is to be continuous. This is done by using a simple process structure at all levels of the organization, from micro to macro. Every process from every perspective must have this structure. Within this organization, both man and machine are completely integrated in order to effect robustness, the ability to converge resources and processes on the quality product at all times. This book describes the road to quality in a dynamic environment.

The structures advocated in these chapters follow sound engineering principles, but the descriptions are in everyday business language. You don't need to be an engineer to read this book, but you do need to believe that it is possible to maintain dynamic consistency and stability whatever the environment. This book is for the implementors.

William A. Stimson

A C K N O W L E D G M E N T S

If I have seen further it is by standing on the shoulders of giants.

Isaac Newton, 1676

Writing a book about what you believe takes a certain amount of ego. You must believe, first, that you are right, and second, that someone cares. Writing a book is also a humbling experience because you must acknowledge, in your heart of hearts, that your belief stems from the knowledge of others, of which, perhaps, you have extended this wisdom a microscopic amount. If Newton was humbled, then those of us far, far down the list are humbled indeed.

We might, for the sake of argument, say that life can be viewed from two perspectives: the strategic or the tactical—the big picture or the detail. I propose a third: the systems viewpoint—the consideration of both the big picture *and* the detail. This proposal would be almost trivial except that the ability to achieve the systems perspective is so difficult. Many have succeeded. Among the foremost of them was Jack Gibson of the Systems Engineering Department, School of Engineering, the University of Virginia.

John Egan Gibson was an engineer, professor, entrepreneur, lifelong student, and warm human being, all of the first rank. A renown authority on nonlinear systems, he moved into the arena of large business and social systems in the 1960s, along with many of his peers. But whereas many of these theorists found that the world was underwhelmed by their considerations and returned to their ivory towers, Jack just tightened his belt and went to work. He studied business processes. He learned the vocabulary of commerce and industry. He wrote books and papers about how to "engineer" the industrial organization. To the end of his life, Jack was in the forefront of thought, teaching quality function deployment and reengineering before these ideas even had names. I benefited from this man's largesse for a quarter of a century before I ever met him, having studied under his former students. At last we met and friendship began. We were of a similar age, religion, and ethnic background, and shared a tendency to laugh at the same things. Alas, God called him Home all too soon. I miss him.

Other far thinkers must be recognized. I wish to thank Doug McAvoy and Ross Cohen of the Naval Ship Weapon Systems Engineering Station, Port Hueneme, California, for their own broad views and their challenge to me to widen my own. Dragoslav Šiljak of Santa Clara University helped me to think nonlinearly and was my first role model on how to use local techniques for global applications. Like Jack Gibson, Dr. Šiljak had an immense curiosity of the world about him. Others introduced me to thinking correctly about systems: C. D. Johnson of the University of Alabama, and Larry Gordineer and Frank Kilmer of IBM. Parry Stroud, an English professor at Texas Western College, instilled in me the desire to read widely and reflect about what I read. And there are those who kept me from quitting when the going was not just tough, but awful. Chief among them was Lt. Col. Rick Metro, U.S. Army, who might let you sink twice but never the third time. Rick's specialty, in addition to giving heart, was organizing time, and I've never seen it done better.

My opinion of formal education is that it is mostly hard, lonely, and miserable. That assessment goes across the board, from Sacred Heart Grammar School of Los Angeles to all of the universities that I've attended. There is one exception—a place that you dream about, where learning is a challenge and a positive experience. That place is the Darden Graduate School of Business of the University of Virginia. My initiation into business and industrial operations at Darden was informative, profound, current, and pure pleasure. Although the study was intense, the dedication and professionalism of the faculty made the process what education is supposed to be: a delightful quest for knowledge.

Last and certainly not least is my own family: my wife Josette, and son Patrick, who sustained me in the ups and downs of a turbulent career. I said in the beginning of this acknowledgment that an author must believe in himself. The origin of my belief derives from my wife and son.

William A. Stimson

CONTENTS

Chapter 4

Designing Robust Processes   51

Chapter 5

Process Dynamics   69

Chapter 6

Process Organization   99

Chapter 7

The Measurement Process   115

Chapter 8

Statistical Measurement   143

Chapter 9

Corrective Processes   159

1

⑥ A FEW FUNDAMENTALS

A STRATEGY FOR QUALITY

> Tonsard had a barrel of vin ordinaire, from which, in the morning,
> he filled a few empty bottles and placed them in view on the shelf.
> When a customer came in and asked for a glass of quality wine,
> the innkeeper turned to his wife: "Marie," he said gravely,
> "there's still a bottle or two left, over there, on the shelf."
>
> *Balzac,* Les Paysans

Tonsard, the innkeeper, had organized a process that would produce consistently and efficiently. But despite his claims, he didn't produce quality. His market was aimed at the nondiscriminating. Tonsard could afford to do this because his was an extremely local market: an isolated village. This book is aimed at those who want to produce consistently and efficiently, but who also want to produce a quality product. They want to do this because they find themselves in a global market oriented toward an increasingly discriminating clientele.

We, the readers and I, in the ensuing chapters will study a strategy for the pursuit of a quality product, and develop organizations that will ensure robust processes to that end. In order to do this efficiently, we will want to avoid semantic hang-ups, so when we come to names and terms that might be ambiguous, or that might mean different things to different people, we will adopt a definition on the spot as a convention for progress. The definitions will be intuitive where possible, rigorous where necessary. And we will use another convention, the pronoun "we." This is not for your benefit but for mine. It brings me closer to you and helps me bear in mind that what I write must be clear enough to be understood by others.

AN AGREEMENT ON MEANING

Some years ago, I attended a conference whose objective was to write some specifications for ship repair. It comes as no surprise to those who deal in contracts that a major impediment to word-smithing is to come to an agreement on the meaning of words. During one discussion about conducting testing of electronics equipment, it became unclear whether a test is *run, done,* or *conducted,* and whether these actions are satisfied by physically manipulating things with the hands, or whether there is some cerebral or supervisory requirement. Finally, one exasperated member declared that the way to run a test is to just *do* it. To which another member asked, "What does 'to do' mean?"

We use a lot of words in our everyday conversation and in business discussions where the meanings are specific only to ourselves and only to the particular case at hand. Others in the same conversation may even have a contradictory interpretation. For example, at the ship repair conference, a requirement was put into a specification that for a particularly complex repair job demanding a wide range of skills, at *least* three craftsmen would be needed. It was hoped that this requirement would inhibit low-balling, or underbidding, the job in order to get the contract. As it turned out, all subsequent bids were for *exactly* three craftsmen and the interpretation legally satisfied the requirement, although it defeated its intent.

We will often take an engineering approach to the meaning of words in this book. Engineering word usages are always specific and unique; there is only one meaning with no nuances. We will use the engineering definition of a word where it exists, even though it differs from the popular usage. A case in point is the word *robust,* which is the central idea of this book and which will be explained shortly. So if you come to a word or idea where the meaning is unusual or too narrow for you, bear with us. The purpose of precise meanings is to lessen ambiguity. It's hard to create robust organizations with loose descriptions.

THE ROLE OF ORGANIZATION

You would think that three generations after Frederick Winslow Taylor,[1] the role of organization would be well defined. Quite the opposite is true. Industry has gone from Theory X to Theories Y and Z and beyond. The notion of organization is under considerable attack these days because it is seen by some as an inflexible residue of Taylorism, which is almost universally recognized as outmoded. These days, savants and gurus argue about pyramid structures, centralization, complacency, and vision. Words like reengineering, downsizing, strategic change, and global workspace are thrown about. Companies are warned that change isn't good enough; transformation is really what's required. The idea is promoted that a company must be amorphous in order to compete successfully in the global environment.

Reengineering and *transformation* are the kinds of words that we are talking about. As popularly used, they are not engineering words at all, but are rather ambiguous; however, they do promote major organizational change. It might sound fashionable to say that you are reengineering your company, but if you have been in business awhile, if you already enjoy some success, then some part of your organization is working fine; reengineering must be done with discretion, lest the baby be thrown out with the bath water.

The key word here is *organization.* Organization is essential if you want a repeatable process. The organization must be defined and the way that it is defined also defines the process. Whether the command structure is pyramidal, inverted, horizontal, or vertical is not important as long as the organization is adaptive. Are there two kinds of organizations, one based on command structure and the second based on the production process? Clearly no, because this leads to two well-known lamentations: (1) "It didn't happen on my watch," and (2) "It must've fallen through the cracks." A robust organization will be fully integrated so as to be effective, which means that adaptability has to be thoughtfully built in, in order for spot changes to be made without affecting the whole structure.

The role of organization is to effect a process, which in turn exists to achieve a goal. Any process can be made adaptable if it is dynamic, and here we use an engineering term. A dynamic process is one whose state changes with time. (State, too, has a precise engineering definition, but for our purposes, we can live with an intuitive meaning.[2]) Contrary to popular usage, the changes of state do not have to be high speed in order to be dynamic, but the time constants of detection and correction must be appropriate to those of disturbance.

Consider Figure 1–1. Engineers will quickly recognize this structure as a basic closed-loop system used to provide stability in production processes. Although a technical concept, it is clear from the array of factors listed beside each mechanism that this structure has general application anywhere in the corporation. In fact, something like it is used in many manufacturing and service organizations. This is because the basic closed-loop control system is a fundamental organizational structure, without which stability and repeatability are not possible. Even if you have never heard of closed-loop control, you will still evolve to a similar structure in order to remain successful in business. Nevertheless, two things can be said: (1) It is difficult to keep the loop closed unless you work at it, and (2) it is not robust by itself.

This book is about using organization to achieve robustness; that is, stable, capable processes that adapt to strategic and tactical disturbances, random or otherwise. Engineers have been doing this on the production line for years. The same thing can be done in the same way for the organization at company level.

ROBUSTNESS

What does *robust* mean? *Encyclopaedia Britannica* defines it this way: "(1) Possessing or characterized by great strength or endurance; rugged; healthy. (2) Requiring strength. (3) Violent, rude." These various interpretations suggest that the essence of robustness is strength. Following a violation by Serb forces against Bosnian forces during a United Nations mandated truce in the latter part of 1994, the U.N. delivered an air strike against a Serb airfield. The strike was labeled "robust" by the U.N., which indicates the generally accepted understanding of the word. But in the

F I G U R E   1–1

The Structure of a Typical Production Process

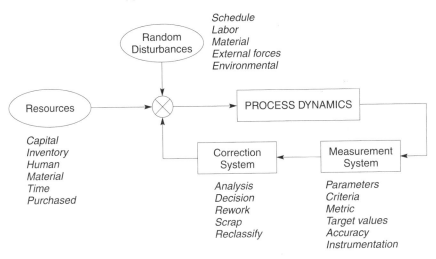

technical world, *robust* has a different, specific meaning. The word is used in a number of engineering applications in optimum design, statistics, and designing for quality. Let's review this use in these various applications, in order to determine what this commonly understood characteristic is.

In engineering, optimum design is an iterative process. You formulate the desired system and determine appropriate design variables. You relate these variables in a cost function of some sort, then vary parameters to find the optimum value of the cost function, if it exists. Algorithms are used to do this optimization. *Robust* refers to the certainty with which an algorithm, starting from an arbitrary point, will converge to an optimum value of the cost function. Among robust algorithms, those that converge faster than others are considered more robust. Thus, *robustness* refers to the rapidity and certainty of convergence.

In statistics, the objective is to characterize an uncertain process, usually by determining the mean value and variation of a parameter of interest. *Robust* refers to the degree to which a statistical technique approximates a theoretically normal distribution. For example, a discrete binomial distribution is robust for a large sample size, no matter what its single-shot probability. Robustness is important because the normal distribution is well defined, so that if a random process is robust, then with only a modest amount of data we can make very accurate judgments about its mean and variance.

In quality engineering, the objective is to design a product so that a key parameter will maintain its optimal value despite environmental factors or random disturbances. *Robust* means that the functional characteristics of the product will be at their target value and remain insensitive to variations in noise factors, that is, changes in the environment.

All three definitions imply the characteristic of *convergence* of a parameter or process from some arbitrary value, behavior, or deviation to a desired value or behavior. This idea is the one that will be used in this book. Thus, *robustness* is that quality of a process that converges to a target value, behavior, or objective, then maintains that target, irrespective of disturbance. The target value may change. The ability to track a moving target is a necessary feature for improvability. A robust process will *track and maintain* a target value. The tenet of this book is that robustness can be built into a process by appropriate organization.

THE ROBUST STRUCTURE

Let's understand robustness. Figure 1–2 shows a "quality loss" curve, indicating that cost can increase nonlinearly as a process deviates from a target value or objective. The idea of paying an increasing penalty as quality degrades is reasonable but still novel; many companies consider that any deviation from target is equally acceptable until tolerance limits are exceeded. Most quality engineers agree, however, that quality losses increase steeply in some arbitrary way, their form depending upon the company, the market, the product, and the type and number of processes through which the product passes. This experience is reflected in the figure. For very small deviation the penalty, too, is small, but then increases sharply several times, finally tapering off toward some maximum cost.

Figure 1–2 should be regarded in a general sense. The "t" on the abscissa can mean target value, or time, or any independent

F I G U R E   1–2

A Nonlinear Quality Loss Function

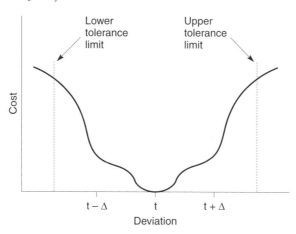

variable. The cost can refer to cost of production, labor, material, administration, decision, morale, or any dependent variable. This curve can represent deviation in *any* process or organization.

The importance of the quality loss concept is that it provides convergence to a target value in designing a system, and it provides sensitivity to deviation in an operating system. The idea is not confined to purely mechanical processes, but is applicable to man-in-the-loop systems as well. Carried to a logical conclusion, it can be descriptive of responses to managerial decisions as well as to engineering design, so that the functions of design and planning are similar. Thus, a robust system will lead to convergence to the objective of a planned activity.

Robustness is a quality of operation that must be planned, or designed, into a process. The company that wants to achieve a robust operation must also be able to achieve a robust design. For example, the methods of Genichi Taguchi (1990) focus on the *design* of product and process from the customer's viewpoint, to create a *robust* product. Taguchi methods, when applied to a design process, are called *off-line quality control.* When applied to working systems, they are called *on-line quality control.* The same organization can be used for both.

Thus, the robust system is robust from day one. You design it, or plan it, to achieve a target objective, and you design it to maintain that target during process operation. Finally, you design it so that the target value itself can change. Nothing is fixed except the basic structure of the organization. This is robustness.

The core idea of the robust organization is shown in Figure 1–3. There are a few more blocks of activity here than in the basic feedback structure of Figure 1–1, but this is not the main difference. The major idea here is that the production process cannot be considered in isolation from the overall company structure. Planning and design,[3] operation, and dynamic correction are *integrated* processes.

The improvement subsystem is the heart of the adaptive process and gives an important added dimension to the robustness of the overall system. By definition, a robust system will converge to a desired objective. The improvement subsystem, properly designed, accommodates a change in the objective also, so that the entire system is in dynamic equilibrium.

Improvement processes are so important that a chapter will be devoted to the subject, but while examining Figure 1–3 it is worth noting that detection is an important factor in improvement, thus the feedforward and feedback to the subsystem. This detection differs from the measurement subsystem in this way. Detection in the sense of improvement is a macro activity, whereas measurement is a micro activity. Measurement tells us whether our *product* is deviating from target value. Detection tells us whether the *process* will produce an off-target product as a result of differences between forecasting and current market forces, or because of random disturbances. Current market forces include changes in customer perceptions and requirements. Both detection and measurement subsystems feed into the planning and design systems in order to change any subprocesses as necessary, including target objectives.

THE ELEMENTS OF QUALITY

Some things cannot be quantified or rigorously defined: fine art or good wine, for example. Our sense of these things is best left to the heart and intuition. Still, we study about these things if only to be able to say why we like some art or a certain wine, and in order to

FIGURE 1–3

A Robust-Capable Structure

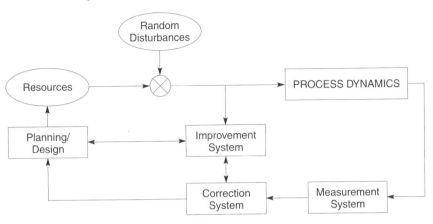

better appreciate them. And so it is with quality. Mostly, our sense of quality is intuitive. Without being able to define quality or measure it, we know it when we see it. Intuition has been the basis for judging quality throughout the ages, and probably still is.

But in the age of manufacturing, it is important to do what hasn't been done—to measure quality so that we can produce it over and over again, perhaps thousands of items that may have taken generations to produce in another age. And you can't measure something until you've defined it. So attempts are made to both define and measure quality, which doesn't strip the customer of his traditional right to his own preferences, but does allow the manufacturer to estimate those customer preferences and mass produce them.

So to begin, we need a workable definition of quality. It is not as easy as you might think; there are important nuances of difference among the most widely used definitions. Artemis March (1986) discussed the definitions used by the three leading quality gurus: W. Edwards Deming, Joseph Juran, and Philip Crosby. Briefly, their respective definitions of quality are "continuous improvement," "fitness for use," and "conformance to requirements." These ideas are at least concise. The definition used by the International Organization for Standardization (ISO) is at the same time more expansive and abstract. Put briefly, it is an integration of properties that satisfy customer needs. All the definitions have varying degrees of subtlety, but the most utilitarian is that of Crosby. It can be brought to bear directly upon service industries, but is less useful in manufacturing. The reason is that workers on the factory floor, who are, in the end, responsible for a quality product, never get to see the customer requirements. All they ever see are the specifications of the job order. For our purposes, then, we will adapt the Crosby definition slightly and define quality to be "conformance to specifications." This definition is not written in stone; you can modify it if you wish, but it gives us some common ground to allow conversation on the subject.

Measuring quality is usually done in this way. We don't measure what it is, but what it isn't. That is, customer desires are determined, and from them a product is designed along with a process that can make the product. Then *deviation* from the designed ideal is measured.

The manufacturer wants to make a good product and then do it over and over again. However, we make measurements in reverse order—we first measure whether the productive process can do something over and over again, then we measure how good it is. The first characteristic is called stability, and the second is called capability. Finally, we want the product to be continuously improvable, which implies more than the ability to make the same product better and better. It implies the ability to follow the desires of the customer, or in other words, to be able to shoot at a moving target.

Stability, capability, and improvability are the basic elements of the quality process. We will talk more about them throughout this book. All of the strategies, transformations, changes, reorganizations, claims for success, and sheer managerial pandemonium have to be translated into stability, capability, and improvability, if the company is to build a quality product.

WHERE WE'RE GOING

For our purposes, an organization is an arrangement or structure of processes. It is this organization that we want to make robust, but of course, the processes must be robust also, because they themselves have a structure. In many cases, the processes will be machines, and properly selected, they will already be robust. But we don't want to fix on the idea that a process is a machine. The purchasing department provides a process—it purchases. The same is true of marketing, operations, customer relations, and every department that you have, including production. The production process is much more than the sum of its machines; the totality forms a system that is synergistic if there is to be any point to it.

In this book, we talk about reengineering the company for robustness, whether the company is in manufacturing or service. We need a general picture of a corporate system to do this, and Figure 1–3 will be our guide. Each block represents a general subsystem of the company and is a human–mechanism entity. The mechanism may be a machine, a database, a procedure, an activity. For example, the "process dynamics" block of the figure might be an assembly line, but it also might be a purchasing department or the entire company. The whole company must be organized for robustness at all levels—micro and macro; organizing each subsystem into a robust process is necessary but not sufficient. Our approach, then, is to analyze each of the blocks of Figure 1–3 in subsequent chapters, starting with the planning block, and ending with a fully integrated, robust system. There is an added benefit to generalizing our approach—we are forced to use our imagination, to think about how a given process or procedure might fit within our own specific situations. So although our approach is systematic, this is not a book on how to get robustness *by the numbers*.[4] You must think about how these ideas might be applied to your own processes.

As thinking precedes action, we begin with corporate philosophy, the driving force of quality planning. Then, block by block of Figure 1–3, we go through each element, discuss the engineering and organizational concepts, and show how a robust structure is *implemented* in the corporate organization.

N O T E S

1. **Frederick Winslow Taylor.** Taylor was a late-19th-century industry analyst, generally considered to be the father of scientific management. For example, he initiated time and motion studies. The labor

force at that time was largely populated by immigrants with rudi-
mentary education and command of the English language. Either for
this reason, or because it was his nature, Taylor recommended
paternal and authoritarian roles for management. This style is now
called *Taylorism* and is in disrepute in the modern era.

2. **State.** The notion of *state* is primitive; that is, we can accept an
intuitive concept, or if we wish to define it, then we must use other
primitive notions to do so. In fact, this is what systems engineers do.
For example, DeRusso et al. (1965) declare that the idea of state is a
fundamental concept and, therefore, cannot be defined; then the
authors proceed to define it in terms of a system of state variables,
themselves only implicitly defined. Typical of this implicit sort of
definition is one provided by Cadzow and Martens (1970): "We
define a *system* as a mathematical abstraction that utilizes three types
of variables to represent or model the dynamics of a process. The
three variables are called input, output, and *state* variables . . . The
state variables characterize the internal dynamics of the system . . .
For a given process, the state variable representation is not unique."
An explicit, intuitive definition of state, taken from Stimson (1988), is
the following: "The state of a system is an internal attribute at the
present moment which determines the present output and affects
future outputs." Abraham and Ledolter (1983) point out that the basis
of state space is the Markov property, which implies the independence
of the future of a process from its past, given the present state. In a
Markov system, the state of a process summarizes all the information
from the past necessary to predict the future.

3. **Planning and Design.** These concepts are shown as a single block in
Figure 1–3, not because they are synonyms but because they are
similar functions. One of the purposes of this book is to get managers
to think like engineers, and to get engineers to think like managers.
One way to do this is to show the similarities in what they do. Nevertheless, one cannot generalize away that which is commonly accepted.
In the language, although there is great overlap in the meanings of the
two words, there are also many nuances associated with them, so that
they are complementary. And in business, they are regarded as
different activities. In general, the planning department does not do
design, nor conversely. Industry interprets the two notions narrowly
and distinctly. We accept this reality and treat planning and design in
two different chapters. However, careful reading of the two chapters
shows that planners design, and designers plan.

4. **By the Numbers.** Most people are probably familiar with this term. Young Army recruits do mass activities such as drill by the numbers literally—for example, the command "Count off, by the numbers!" We have seen numbered painting outlines in which each number represents a particular color to be used. The idea of doing things by the numbers suggests a mindless mechanism by which someone of little skill can achieve an objective. Yet, the method is used in supposedly skilled environments. Some years ago, I attended a training course in project management analysis, in which the class was taught how to analyze by the numbers. The process was tedious beyond description. I believe that the *by the numbers* idea originates in a human tendency to pedagogy and it is pervasive. I also believe that it doesn't appeal to the American way of doing things, at least it doesn't appeal to mine. That is why I avoid formal descriptions of brainstorming and Quality Function Deployment in this book.

REFERENCES

Abraham, Bovas; and Johannes Ledolter. *Statistical Methods for Forecasting*. New York: John Wiley & Sons, 1983.

Balzac, Honoré de. *Les Paysans*. Paris: Éditions Garnier Fréres, 1964.

Cadzow, James A., and Hinrich R. Martens. *Discrete-Time and Computer Control Systems*. Englewood Cliffs, NJ: Prentice Hall, 1970.

DeRusso, Paul M.; Rob J. Roy; and Charles M. Close. *State Variables for Engineers*. New York: John Wiley & Sons, 1965.

March, Artemis. "A Note on Quality: The Views of Deming, Juran, and Crosby." *Harvard Business School Note* 9-687-011, 1986; rev 2/90, pp. 1–13.

Stimson, William A. "Principles of Systems Testing." *Naval Engineers Journal*, November 1988, pp. 48–58.

Taguchi, Genichi, and Don Clausing. "Robust Quality." *Harvard Business Review*, January–February 1990, pp. 65–75.

2

⑥ DYNAMIC THINKING

THINKING

I beseech you, in the bowels of Christ Jesus, think it possible that you might be mistaken.

Oliver Cromwell to the Church of Scotland, 1650

Cromwell's challenge is cogent to us because, although thinking is natural to humans, thinking well is not, and thinking about change is even harder. You might wonder, given his reputation, why quote Cromwell? There are great thinkers in history and his name is not among them. Why not quote the great ones? In fact, there are three good reasons to turn our attention to this man. The first is that the quote is appropriate. Our challenge is to rethink our understanding about industry and about quality. Second, if the conduct of arms requires thought, and I believe that it does, then Cromwell has few peers in thinking about his profession, which is as much as you can say about anyone. Third, the great thinkers in history are regarded as philosophers, and although businessmen should have a philosophy about what they do (and we approach this idea in the next chapter), their objective is not philosophy but business.

Those who work for a living find few moments in which to think. The demands of the marketplace are insatiable. Often we think on weekends, which means the time for thinking about our business affairs is subtracted from our family time, but that's the way it is. Five years ago, realizing that I had lost control of my program, and that I faced increasingly dissatisfied customers, I left my job to return to school, to find some time to think.

You can think either by yourself or in a group. You ought to do both. You establish what it is you believe about yourself, your profession, your industry, or your product only in the privacy of your own mind. You determine what more you need to learn. You cannot decide where to go or what your goal in life is until this private confrontation has taken place. But we work in groups, for a company. The purpose and direction of the group must be a collective determination, first of all because everyone is invested in the enterprise, and second, because collective wisdom is superior to individual wisdom. In the group, each individual's best ideas can be used, poor ideas identified and abandoned, and breadth of expertise expanded. This chapter is about systematic ways to achieve thinking.

THINKING ABOUT CHANGE

Dynamic thinking precedes dynamic planning.[1] Planning is thinking with goals in mind, but thinking is the essential skill. There are four independent elements that determine *how* we think: abstraction, logic, breadth, and depth. Most people excel in one or more; few excel in all of them. A person is often characterized by his strong suit. We might say, "How easily he gets the big picture," or "She's so logical." However, we are not going to pursue these elements, which are either inherent in us or not. Instead, whatever our capabilities, we want to think about *what* to think about. And what to think about is change.[2] At first blush this seems to be a motherhood statement. After all, everybody thinks about change. Or do they? Let's examine some of the characteristics about the way we think and compare them to characteristics about the way things change.

> *Every body continues in its state of rest, or of uniform motion in a right line, unless it is compelled to change that state by forces impressed upon it.*

Newton's first law is studied in every physics class, but it is revealing to call physics by its former name—natural philosophy. This leads to a tantalizing idea, that nature not only resists physical change, but also resists *metaphysical* change. In other words, Newton's first law is true of all bodies, including bodies without mass, such as our minds.

Is there any evidence to support this idea, that we tend to think in constant terms, to retain fixed concepts? A simple review of some old saws that we hear every day indicates that we do:

"It's not in our charter."

"That's not my job."

"If we can just hold a steady course . . ."

"Judging from the past, . . ."

Thinking about change is not easy, and when we do think about it, our tendency is to think of linear change. But the behavior of events in business (and most activities) is often nonlinear, and if we want to stay ahead of the power curve, so to speak, then we need to think nonlinearly, too. Dynamic thinking, then, means not only being able to accommodate the changes in reality with proportionate changes in concept, but to *anticipate these changes*. And that must be done both strategically and tactically.

Thinking about change means the ability to perceive when change is occurring about us, and it helps to do that if we are familiar with some of the common ways in which change occurs. Some years ago, in the combat information center aboard a cruiser of the United States Navy, it was my privilege to participate in a missile exercise, the interception of a "vandal," an enemy threat simulated by a supersonic drone. Although we had never engaged a supersonic threat before, the crew and I had much experience with subsonic targets and believed ourselves prepared to shoot down the new threat as soon as our radars picked it up.

When a threat is detected and acquired, the engagement systems assign a video marker on the scopes that points in the direction in which the threat is heading, and has length in proportion to the speed of the target. The length assigned to this supersonic threat was so long that we stared at it in disbelief. The gunnery officer concluded, "My scope is misadjusted, dammit!" We almost lost the window of opportunity in the time it took to accept the new reality.

I tell this story to demonstrate that we see what we expect to see, and that in order to see what is really there, it helps to have some idea of what is probable. In theory, change can take any form of behavior, but we will exclude the pathological on the grounds that this is chaos, and business is rarely chaotic,[3] despite the present fashion of saying so. Figure 2–1 shows a number of behavior profiles, that is, ways in which things can change. By increasing our perception of the way things can change, we expand the limits on thinking about it.

The step of Figure 2–1(d) is a mathematical abstraction; there can be no instantaneous change. Change takes a finite time to occur. Nevertheless, a change can be *perceived* as a step. For example, the breakdown of an assembly line machine can cause a nearly instantaneous change in quality. Thus, in the physical world, the ramp of Figure 2–1(b) and the step of Figure 2–1(d) are related, because the ramp can have any slope, so that the step may be regarded as a ramp with very steep slope. This analogy is useful because it widens the view of radical change. In software engineering, for example, program defects are detected as a ramp function throughout the development process. However, defects occur as a step function; that is, most of them are put into the process early on. Delineating fault creation and detection as two different functions stresses the need for heavy quality programs up front.

The last inset, Figure 2–1(f), is not a profile of the behavior of change, but is an example of the probability that a change will take place. This example displays a well-behaved variation, with high probability of no change, and equally likely probabilities of increase or decrease. The idea of understanding change behaviors in terms of their time profiles is scarcely new; forecasters attempt to build predictive models of change as a regular part of their analyses. The point here is that dynamic analysis is not just for the technocrat but is a necessary management capability.

The occurrence of change has various profiles partly because of the rate of natural events and partly because of the reluctance of humanity to recognize change. Lowenthal (1994) calls change a slow and sometimes painful process, and points out that major inventions such as gunpowder, the printing press, and the facsimile machine were ignored by whole populations for years. He adds that today change is no longer slow, as word of new technologies travels quickly. This supports the view of Toffler (1970), and explains why dealing with change is one of the foremost issues of our day.

FIGURE 2–1

Some Examples of Change Behavior: (a) Constant Behavior (No Change);
(b) Ramp; (c) Exponential or Geometric; (d) Step; (e) Sinusoidal; (f) Normally Distributed Probability of Change

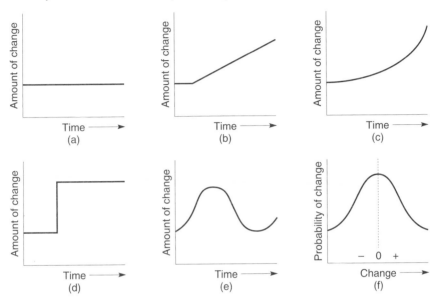

From the point of view of industrial organizations, there are two kinds of change: those that act on us and those that we initiate. Whether reactive or initiative, the change is usually tactical unless a goal is involved. Having established goals, we may initiate a change in *process* in order to arrive at them, but external forces acting upon us may bring about a strategic reaction: a need to change one or more *goals*. For example, a shift in customer desires may require a change in goals, and a consequent change in the production systems used to satisfy those desires. We try to anticipate customer desires with market analysis, but whether driven by initiative or reaction, we are interested in getting customer requirements into the production system in a timely way. In order to effect this change, the production processes need to be adaptable.

The ability to quickly effect change in a production process is a hallmark of a robust organization. Most management have no difficulty with initiative; if they do, they won't be managers long.

The difficulty comes in dealing with change that acts upon us. Management usually consider that this means change due to external forces, because it is assumed that internal forces are under control. In fact, there is one kind of internal change that many managers ignore, and that is *variation*. It is random and undesirable, and being a natural phenomenon, it is inevitable. It goes on all the time. Variation, too, is mostly a management responsibility, although many managers do not understand this. Moreover, it is common among managers to underestimate the breadth of variation in their processes and to misinterpret its nature.

> *A fault in the interpretation of observations is to suppose that every event (defect, mistake, accident) is attributable to someone, or is related to some special event. The fact is that most troubles with service and production lie in the system.*

If we think carefully about the words of W. Edwards Deming, we will realize that variation occurs in all our processes, not just those engaged directly in production. Moreover, it is inherent in any system that we set up. Deming (1991) uses the term *common causes* to describe systematic faults causing variation, and the term *special causes* to describe fleeting events. He estimates that 94 percent of common causes are the responsibility of management to eliminate. Juran (1992) puts the figure at between 80 percent and 90 percent, so there is general agreement about the evidence of management responsibility to this kind of change also.

Common causes limit what the production system can do repeatedly. Even if customer desires change gradually, it is possible that requirements to meet that change may eventually exceed the capability of the production system. This may not show up right away as an inherent production limitation. On the contrary, it may appear as a problem in production. Management personnel who are unfamiliar with statistical control can lose valuable time against the competition here by assigning the problem to equipment troubleshooters, when the real problem is systematic and must be resolved by the managers themselves.

Some examples were given earlier of frequently made statements that indicate fixed views and aspirations, and linear thinking. But change often occurs nonlinearly, and the longer the term of consideration, the more likely is nonlinear change. This is why dynamic thinking considers both the near-term and long-term horizon. In the near term, we can often linearize how change might affect our plans, but in the long term, this sort of thinking can lead to major error. Long- and short-term perceptions each have their own characteristics. We'll discuss some of these, and in doing so, find ways to be dynamic about strategic and tactical thinking.

Tactical Thinking

The present moment dominates our lives. We confront this reality with short-term thinking, oriented toward what is happening now or expected soon. In considering what can happen soon, we can "linearize" our perspective in order to make bottom-up plans in preparation. Linearization[4] means that we assume, given a short enough period of time, that the world won't change much. In terms of the change profiles of Figure 2–1, we expect that 2–1(a), or 2–1(b) with modest slope, will pertain. This simplifies the range of what we need to think about, but can be justified only through experience. If, within the context of the quality under considera-tion, past environments have never provided a sudden, great per-turbation, then it is reasonable to limit our thoughts to the range of things that have happened.

Linearization allows us to make straightforward judgments about how many employees to use on a given shift or assembly line section and how many units to hold in inventory or to pro-duce in a given season. Forecasting is easier, also, because the error in overestimation is the same as in underestimation; we accept a penalty magnitude that we can live with, knowing that it will be the same whether we guess over or under, and go for it.

There is nothing new in the idea of linearized thought. In fact, we do it even when we shouldn't. There are two caveats to lin-earized thought. The first is what is meant by "short term." Here again, we can rely on experience. The short term is defined as that period of time, or increment of state, in which, according to the past, only small changes will occur. Often, it is wise to assign prob-abilities to these changes, as in Figure 2–1(f). This tactic is the basis of control charting. Systematic variation is defined as that variation within .9973 probability limits. Since systematic variation must be lived with, it is acceptable, and therefore "small." Linearization is properly used, then, by defining the period of time or range of state variables over which we can expect, with high probability, that changes in state are predictable and small.

The second caveat is sensitivity of the issue about which we assume changes will be linear and small. Sensitivity analysis examines what will happen if we're wrong about a given issue. What would it cost you if there is a sudden increase of competition, loss of customer interest, or assembly line failure? So we assume linear behavior profiles on relatively insensitive issues over a short period of time. Otherwise, we need to widen expectations in our tactical thinking.

Strategic Thinking

Strategy comes from the Greek "strategos," referring to the general's art. Strategic thinking is about the big picture, the long term. It considers the global behavior of the state of a system. Michel Robert, founding partner of Decision Process International, says that strategic thinking begins by identifying the company's driving force and areas of excellence (Kinni, 1994). For the moment, let's adopt an intuitive notion of "driving force" as what the company is all about. Beyond these concepts, though, we must add a consideration of both the company's global environment, and its internal self. We can then use these concepts to arrive at cohesive goals and a direction for the company that all its employees can participate in. Knowing the areas of excellence, we delineate what we can do well in the face of competition. Knowing the global environment, we qualitatively identify potential forces of change. *Internal self* is the human, moral composition of the company and refers to the degree to which employees identify their own interests with that of the company. Some companies kid themselves about this; others don't care. They are not visionary. There can be little cohesive direction of the company if there is little cohesion among the employees; we shall discuss this subject at greater length in a later chapter. In sum, strategic thinking pursues free-ranging thoughts about things that might be with respect to company, customer, and the internal and external environment.

In discussing visionary companies, Jim Collins and Jerry Porras (1994), of Stanford University, define a company's driving force as its core ideology, which should be the basis of its strategic thinking. They point out that long-term successful companies have a raison d'être that changes seldom, if ever. This sense of purpose goes beyond just making money. However, at the same time, the successful company stimulates improvement, innovation, and renewal in everything that is not core value. Once you're clear as to what is to remain fixed and sacred, then you are free to change everything else about the organization in order to achieve quality.

A core ideology is necessary but not sufficient to a quality company. Also necessary is the *integration* of this philosophy into the fabric of the organization: mission, policies, goals, processes, procedures, functions, management, employees, and structures. This complete integration achieves two things. First, it strengthens the internal self. Second, it necessarily achieves quality function deployment (small letters). In this context it is called total quality management. How the integration is implemented is the subject of dynamic processes discussed in a later chapter. I use small letters because Quality Function Deployment (QFD) is a commonly used name for a rigorous quality methodology.[5] QFD is not germane to this book, but the deployment of the quality function throughout the organization is. This book is about guidelines that are sufficiently flexible that any company can implement them.

IMPLEMENTATION

How do you implement thinking? After all, we either think or we don't. But what we really mean here is how do you implement dynamic thinking into a robust organization? We are interested in the speculative thinking of Aquinas, and want to be free of constraints, to be creative. Creativity isn't done on demand, contrary to the "publish or perish" mandate of research universities, but it can be stimulated by a proper environment.

John F. Kennedy is quoted as telling a group of Nobel Prize winners who were his dinner guests that they were the greatest assembly of thinkers ever to have dined in the White House, with the possible exception of when Thomas Jefferson dined alone.[6] Jefferson's accomplishments in the arena of creative thought scarcely need to be recounted here, but even his ideas often underwent significant modification by others before signature.[7] Even great thinkers need group thinking if the result of the thoughts is to have group application. In Jefferson's case, group thinking served to put limits on a boundless mind. In most cases, group thinking can help to remove limits from bounded minds.

Since the company is the beneficiary of the thinking, it is natural to establish forums of thought from members of the company. We won't presume to tell management how to hold management meetings, but such meetings use only a small part of the knowledge base of the company. In particular, the know-how in quality control and much valuable tactical insight reside within every company at a lower level than management—the first-level supervisors and the workers themselves.

How you put together a forum to exploit this reservoir of ideas in a constructive way is not easy. We maintain social hierarchies in the corporate structure, and groups tend to form within these hierarchies. There are two dangers in hierarchal grouping. The first is that there can be little pollenization between those who are in the best position for tactical thinking and those who are in the best position for strategic thinking. The second is that hierarchies don't sit well with Americans; they create resentment because they are simply a class structure. Ideas that are handed down from a higher level to a lower level are often met with benign neglect or malicious compliance. The failure of quality circles to catch on in American industry in the 1960s can be blamed on the lack of representation within them of all social levels within the organization.

Quality circles are coming back again because they make an excellent forum for creative thought, when organized correctly. They are often called by different names so as not to suffer by association with the failure of the attempts of the past: quality teams, participative management, employee–management teams, and productivity circles, to name a few. Richard Vaughn (1990) lists some requirements for a successful quality circle:

1. Active participation by management.
2. Knowledge of participants of quality control techniques and company operations.
3. Membership of flexible participants.
4. Subsidization by the company.

Item 1 is needed to provide and demonstrate leadership. Mandated quality programs don't work. Employees must be shown that management will participate in a "do as I do" effort. The chairman doesn't have to be the CEO, but should be high enough in rank that he is identified with the front office. This shows the employees that quality is not just another drill, but that high-level management is committed to it and will put its resources into it. People often say that quality is free. It is not. Quality happens only when all involved put mind and conscience into what they are doing. That tends to happen in a team effort, due to peer pressure.

Item 2 ensures that the meetings will be constructive. Almost everyone can contribute to a meeting on how to achieve quality, but contributions are more likely by those who have a broad understanding of what the company does and their part in it. At the beginning of the meetings, some of the first-time participants will tend to turn them into "bitch sessions." While a few minutes of time can be sacrificed to this end, it is the chairman's job to control the direction of discussion. Most employees have a sense of responsibility, and when the purpose of the meeting is made clear to them, and the fact that their own contribution is not only desired but considered necessary for success, then they will join in wholeheartedly.

Item 3 admits reality. Some members of a quality forum either cannot rise to the occasion, cannot conceive of new scenarios, or cannot face the changes that may be suggested. They will fight hard for the status quo. This is one of the reasons for which the participation of higher-level management is needed. Successful processes are closed loop at the tactical level; changes in the environment are often not apparent, and the worker may be unaware of them. At a higher level, the strategist studies the environment. Sometimes all that it takes to get a recalcitrant worker to accept or even to generate new ideas is to make him aware that the environment is changing. Persons who cannot accept the idea of change cannot be used in a quality forum, although their ideas can still be useful in a suggestion system that doesn't require councils.

Item 4 means that the meetings should be on company time. There is something magnificently naïve about the phrase "from each according to his ability; to each according to his needs." Part of the failure of communism is its absolute dependence on continual, unflagging sacrifice by those willing to do so, in compensation for those unwilling. Part of the success of the Constitution is that it is designed to work even when everyone is pursuing his own interests. Item 4 is an admission that it is probably naïve to expect people to sacrifice their own time in the interest of quality. Pay them for it. Employees will respond in a responsible way, knowing that they are being paid for their thoughts.

There are some general considerations of structure concerning quality forums. The number of participants, frequency and location of meetings, and *breadth* of participating company operations are variables that cannot be dictated here but are uniquely determined according to the needs of each company and purpose of the specific meeting. The *depth* of participation should not be a variable. There must be vertical representation and participation from high-level management to floor worker.

Some companies have found success with a simple network of forums. At the highest level, a quality steering committee is formed, composed of upper management and chaired by the president. The purpose of the steering committee is suggested by its name—it considers only strategic questions and provides uniform direction of quality issues across the company. This uniformity of direction is achieved in this way: each member of the steering committee serves as chairman of lower-level quality forums, horizontally distributed. This provides vertical integration of ideas. Quality function deployment (horizontal integration) is achieved by overlapping organizational structure in the composition of the forum membership.

There are other forum structures, to be sure. Some experts advocate the use of facilitators at meetings, under the assumption that some managers often lack the skills needed to manage team discussions.[8] The company with such leaders is in far deeper trouble than its inability to hold forums. Having facilitators as co-chairmen of a forum always reminds me of a Soviet council, in which a party functionary had to be there to make sure that the leader was not preaching revisionism. If you have a manager who is not a good facilitator, then train him to be one. It never pays to confuse team members about who the leader is.

Given the forum, there are a number of ways in which to generate thought; the best way will depend upon the objective. In the Aquinas theme, that is, speculative thinking, Gibson (1990) suggests a few: brainstorming, brainwriting, and options fields. In pure brainstorming, there are no imposed limits and no criticism is tolerated until time for critique. Every idea is put on the table for serious discussion. Entertaining unlimited, even irresponsible or irrelevant ideas is the best way to break out of the mold of incremental change, into a world different in kind. Brainstorming requires abandonment of inhibitions, and to encourage that, the forum should be conducted away from the plant, in a very informal setting, with informal dress code and conduct. This format is costly and, although important, should not be used too often.[9]

Nevertheless, a modified brainstorming format can be used in-house, on a routine basis, even with management present. The basis of success is to encourage free expression and, above all, no one pulls rank. As in regular brainstorming, only first names are used. We all understand the need for rank formality in the military; you may one day be required to order subordinates into harm's way, and you can't do that if a familiar relationship exists between you. So in the military, a general is always called General. He pays dearly for it in terms of filtered information. On the other hand, Bill Hewlett was always called Bill by his employees; Dave Packard was always called Dave. This wasn't done to be democratic, it was done to break down barriers. You can't make good management decisions if your people are only going to tell you what they think you want to hear.

Brainstorming forums are often taken over by the extroverts in the group. Brainwriting inputs should be encouraged for those who prefer to think before speaking, or who can't function well in the rapid-fire environment of brainstorming. Usually, the brainwriter will present a fairly well-developed idea. At some point this idea should be the subject of a quality forum because it must undergo a baptism of fire, as every other idea. That is precisely the point of brainstorming—a recognition of group wisdom. If the idea is a good one, it will find vigorous defenders no matter the hesitancy of its creator. We can easily imagine the environment of the Constitutional Convention and the composition of the players. Some of them were verbal fighters but not a few were deep thinkers who might have preferred a more tranquil environment. The magnificence of the final product is unchallenged.

Options fields are a format that limits discussion to the topics predetermined in an agenda. Within these constraints, a modified brainstorming format is used. You can say whatever comes to mind, given the subject matter. The topic might be ways to improve in-process inventory, or tool issue. All options are entertained, then critiqued. Options fields thus offer the company a forum that is both open and bounded. It is bounded by the agenda, but within this constraint, it is open by the brainstorming technique to any and all ideas.

We have discussed, briefly, some notions about thinking productively. It begins with an internal examination within ourselves about what we believe and how we want to manifest that belief in our lives and business affairs. We recognize that thinking is fraught with inertia, partly due to comfort with the familiar, partly due to a natural timidity that many of us have about exposing ourselves to ourselves, much less to others. We admit that boldness is required in order to explore the full dimension of our thoughts, and then to share them with others. And share them we must, because business is a social activity. We recognize that the best ideas are tempered in group analysis because there is wisdom in the group, and we have discussed some effective formats for this discussion. From this point, armed with a few ideas, we go on to planning about how to do something constructive with them.

N O T E S

1. **Thinking.** Planning is thinking, too. But the purpose in delineating the two notions here is to liberate pure thinking from the constraints that we place upon it when we plan. The terms are used here in the context expounded by Aquinas in his discussion on two kinds of thinking: *speculative* and *practical*. These two types of thought are of the same power but differ in their objective, the former being the pure consideration of truth; the latter being directed to some particular action.

2. **Change.** The practical person might ask here, "Change in what?" The answer is, change in nothing. The purpose of this discussion is to think about change itself, a consideration that has been going on for

centuries. Philosophers have disagreed about the meaning of change, but mostly their arguments concerned whether motion was involved. For our purposes, *change* means "a transition in state or place."

3. **Chaos.** James Gleick (1987) presents an excellent introductory discussion on chaos. In terms of dynamic systems, chaos can be considered that nonlinear region of state space that contains unstable equilibria. Chaos has high entropy, which means that system behavior is unpredictable and hence unmanageable, at least in the interior of this space. How about managing the boundary conditions? Doug Hutchison writes, in a 1994 issue of *Quality Progress*, that chaotic systems are characterized by a sensitivity to initial conditions that result in unpredictable but orderly final conditions. They are deterministic in the sense that two identical systems perturbed identically will result in the same final state, but the final state is unpredictable from the initial conditions. There are two things to say about this. First, the entropy of a system can be lowered in principle, but the cost may be high. The resources to lower it must be provided continually from an external source. Second, identical systems and sets of initial conditions can be established only in a laboratory, so that the fact that two such systems will result in an identical final state is irrelevant to those who must bet their money on that final state.

4. **Linearization.** In doing nonlinear analysis, engineers will frequently linearize a model about some small neighborhood of a system's equilibrium state, in order to simplify the task of design. The rationale in doing so is based upon an environment of small perturbations. If it is possible that a large perturbation can arrive in the environment, then linearization techniques may not be feasible.

5. **Quality Function Deployment.** QFD is one of the strategies of total quality management originating at the Mitsubishi Kobe shipyard. It's objective is to deploy the voice of the customer horizontally through the processes of planning, engineering, manufacturing, assembly, and service. So far so good. Except that the Japanese do it by the numbers. I don't believe that the rigidity of the process is amenable to American temperament. The objectives and general ideas of QFD should be adopted, but the mechanisms should be suited to local conditions, and above all, they should be as general as possible. I much prefer to use the term in small letters, and let each reader decide for himself how best to deploy the quality function horizontally. See the notes on *By the Numbers* (page 13).

6. **Nobel Prize Dinner, 1962.** According to those who knew him, John F. Kennedy enjoyed holding social events in the White House,

particularly if they presented occasion for good conversation. In 1962
he held a dinner for American Nobel Prize winners, at which he
gave a welcoming presentation. The script was drafted by Arthur
Schlesinger and others, and included the phrase: "This is the greatest
assembly of talent and brains ever assembled in the White House."
Years later, Bobby Kennedy related that JFK added the extempo-
raneous comment to the draft: "except perhaps, when Thomas
Jefferson dined alone." The final form of the quote has become a
favorite of JFK aficionados.

7. **Modifying Jefferson's Ideas.** Jefferson's draft of the Declaration of
Independence suffered significant change by fellow delegates, who
struck out about 25 percent of it completely and altered many words.
Most of this censorship was aimed at making the document less offen-
sive in the hope of gaining independence without war, and thus was
more than wordsmithing, because it represented a different perspective. Other Jefferson documents that were censored or rejected by
fellow delegates at one convention or another were his bill to allow
Virginians to free their slaves, rejected by the House of Burgesses,
1769; his "A Summary View of the Rights of British America," printed,
but not adopted by the Virginia Assembly in 1774 because they felt it
was too radical; and his "An Act for Establishing Religious Freedom,"
passed after modification by the Virginia Assembly, 1779. Except for
the issue of slavery, which he wished to abolish, the power of Jefferson's arguments was so great that the essence of his ideas always
carried the day.

8. **Facilitators.** The idea that leaders may lack the skills to manage teams
effectively in a forum is raised by Longman-Czeropski (1994), in
discussing the rationale for the use of facilitators by many training
professionals. From the tone of her article, this does not seem to be her
own view. On the contrary, she suggests that managers should be
taught facilitating skills, then serve the dual role of leader and
facilitator in forums under their responsibility. This is my view also.

9. **Brainstorming.** This method of generating creativity from a group has
been so successful that it has become a business. There are consultants
in brainstorming. There are *how to* books on brainstorming. The
process can be found described in nitpicky detail, with formal
procedures, facilitators, and so on. (See the notes on *By the Numbers,*
page 13.) You can easily substitute pedagogy for creativity if you
wish, but I believe that brainstorming should remain loosely defined.
Some companies run brainstorming sessions as a New England town
hall meeting. The sessions become a forum for debate and decision

making, attended by a cross section of the company, just as a town meeting is a cross section of the citizenry. The principles of brainstorming sessions are used, suited to local conditions.

REFERENCES

Aquinas, Thomas. *Summa Theologica.* Part VI, Question LXXIX, Article 11, The Great Books. Chicago: Encyclopaedia Britannica, Inc., 1952.

Collins, James C., and Jerry I. Porras. *Built to Last: Successful Habits of Visionary Companies.* New York: Harper Business, 1994.

Churchill, Winston S. *A History of the English Speaking Peoples.* Volume Two, Book V. New York: Dodd, Meade & Company, 1965.

Deming, W. Edwards. *Out of the Crisis.* Cambridge, MA: The Center for Advanced Engineering Study, Massachusetts Institute of Technology, 1991.

Gibson, John E. *How to Do Systems Analysis.* Englewood Cliffs, NJ: Prentice Hall (in review).

Gleick, James. *Chaos: Making a New Science.* New York: Viking Penguin, 1987.

Hutchison, Douglas. "Chaos Theory, Complexity Theory, and Health Care Quality Management." *Quality Progress,* November 1994, pp. 69–72.

Juran, Joseph M. *Juran on Quality by Design.* New York: Copyright © 1992 by Juran Institute, Inc. Published by the Free Press, an imprint of Simon & Schuster.

Kinni, Theodore B. "Find the Corporate Heartbeat." *Industry Week,* August 15, 1994, pp. 43–47.

Longman-Czeropski, Sue. "Follow the Leader." *Quality Progress,* December 1994, pp. 47–49.

Lowenthal, Jeffrey N. *Reengineering the Organization: A Step-by-Step Approach to Corporate Revitalization.* Milwaukee, WI: ASQC Quality Press, 1994.

Toffler, Alvin. *Future Shock.* New York: Random House, 1970.

Vaughn, Richard C. *Quality Assurance.* Ames, IA: Iowa State University Press, 1990.

3

⑥ DYNAMIC QUALITY PLANNING

CORPORATE PHILOSOPHY

In his popular book, *The Goal*, Eli Goldratt's protagonist, Jonah, declares:

> The goal (of a manufacturing organization) is to make money.

Is this true? Jonah goes on to explain that this process can be defined in terms of three criteria: throughput, inventory, and operating expense. Although fiction, Goldratt's book is taken seriously by the business and academic communities. It describes in considerable detail a bottom-up approach to viability of a company in trouble, and this status is achieved by asking, in some cases rather subtly, no other question of a problem on the factory floor than which alternative of several would make the most money.

On the other hand, speaking of a core ideology, Jim Collins and Jerry Porras (1994) say:

> Well, the same principle applies to visionary companies. They have a basic set of core values and a sense of enduring purpose—a reason for existence—that changes seldom, if ever. These values and sense of purpose go far beyond just making money . . .

So who is right? The answer is they both are, but they are positing different arguments. The first was speaking tactically; the second was speaking strategically. Jonah was providing a reference for decision making to a company in trouble, whose problems existed in the present. Collins and Porras were speaking of visionary companies who are preparing for the future. Nevertheless, tactical and strategic decisions within the same company should not conflict. If you want to make a quality product and do it forever, then you come down on the side of a core philosophy, one that you can agree with and that will get you where you want to go.

An excellent definition of company philosophy is found by paraphrasing the words of Hayes and Wheelwright (1984):

> *A set of guiding principles, driving forces, and ingrained attitudes that help communicate quality goals, plans, and policies to all employees and that are reinforced through conscious and subconscious behavior at all levels of the organization.*

This definition ideally suits robust organization because it goes beyond quality policy and quality systems. It includes commitment. The commitment of top management is absolutely required in order to maintain the flexibility to initiate tactical and strategic change. Goldratt points out that "change must be understood as the norm, not as the exception."

The original definition offered by Hays and Wheelwright did not explicitly include quality. Is it necessary? There are companies and government agencies who bandy the word about, but who cannot deliver a quality product or service. There are also companies, such as Metro Machine Corporation of Norfolk, Virginia, who seldom mention the word *quality*, but who consistently provide a quality product. This achievement is in large part due to the president of the company, who is as firmly committed to instilling quality as he is to not talking about it, believing that "once you say you've got quality, it's gone."

In a similar vein, it was probably unnecessary to prohibit the use of titles of nobility in the Constitution, given the first president, but principles meant to endure should be explicit. Commitment to quality may be hard to define, but as the saying goes, "we know it when we see it." A commitment to quality will be obvious in that company whose corporate philosophy includes quality because of the total integration and immersion explicit in the definition. On the other hand, commitment cannot be faked and the company that excludes quality from its philosophy will have weak evidence of quality.

According to Stahl and Grigsby (1928), a company's philosophy is often expressed tersely in a *mission statement,* which is always put in the perspective of the customer. This is not dissembling, even if the company's mission, in its own view, is simply to make money. After all, the most assured way to make money is by satisfying the customer. Hence, mission statements tend to be similar to that of Comdial Corporation of Charlottesville, Virginia: "To build an increasingly profitable, advanced telecommunications systems company through continuing new product development and market diversification, thereby benefiting not only our shareholders, but also our customers and employees."

TOP-DOWN VERSUS BOTTOM-UP

Collins and Porras found that visionary companies invested for the future more than did the others. If so, then the advantage of thinking afar is clear. That's why a large part of the last chapter was devoted to strategic thinking. By Aquinian logic, we can make the same case for strategic, or top-down, planning, because "speculative and practical thinking are of equal power." Much of the literature today concerns strategic planning, given the fall of long-time financial empires, the creation of new ones, and the emergence of a new world order. Almost every company engaged in international trade is doing a great deal of it. The characteristics of strategic planning are well identified and can be found anywhere, and almost always described in commonly accepted terms. These characteristics are fairly constant, no matter what the objective. For example, Juran (1992) shows the striking similarity between strategic *quality* planning and strategic *financial* planning.

Nevertheless, as Peter Drucker says (Tomasko, 1993), sooner or later strategy and the big picture must degenerate into work. Work must be planned, too, not just for today, or for next week, or for the duration of existing contractual requirements, but for an indefinite period of time that we call the intermediate term. In other words, bottom-up planning. Intuitively, you might say that there is a natural, if vague, division between tactical and strategic planning, the latter kicking in beyond the intermediate term, whatever that means. Interestingly, top-down and bottom-up approaches to planning seem to attract mutually exclusive proponents. Some believe that if you do your strategic planning well, the present will take care of itself, given proper organization. On the other hand, some planners endorse bottom-up planning as the more effective.[1]

The delineation of strategic and tactical planning into mutually exclusive camps is brought about because of two very human tendencies. The first is to be pedantic, to sharply define everything (mea culpa). Thus, the terms *strategic planning* and *tactical planning* tend to take on rigid meanings. The second tendency is to divide everything into two camps, "us" versus "them." In this book, we want to use both strategic and tactical planning, and we don't want to expend any energy defending why, or in arguing about what each term means. So we shall use the terms *top-down* and *bottom-up* for strategic and tactical, respectively, because *top-down* and *bottom-up* are intuitive concepts.

Dynamic quality planning (DQP) includes top-down and bottom-up approaches and a comparison of the two will show why. Table 3–1, adapted from Gibson (1990), lists the strengths and weaknesses of each method, and clearly indicates that an effective quality system needs both top-down and bottom-up planning, and must be ongoing, or "dynamic."

PROPERTIES OF DQP

After studying Table 3–1, it becomes clear that top-down and bottom-up planning, although distinct, are not mutually exclusive. They can be used effectively and simultaneously, and even for the same purposes. But they will lead to different objectives. For example, bottom-up planning can provide incremental improvements, but will not lead to an improvement of a completely different kind, as will the top-down approach to planning. Conversely, top-down planning will tell you *where* to go, and maybe *how* to do something, but never in enough detail to make it work. Dynamic quality planning uses both approaches in order to gain the benefits of each, which offset the disadvantages of either. This integration of approaches results in the characteristics of planning

T A B L E   3–1

Comparison of Top-Down and Bottom-Up Planning

Top-Down Planning	
Attributes	Moves from general to specific
	Based on goals and objectives
Strengths	Based on general assumptions and trends in the planning environment
	Identifies changes in the planning environment, and adjusts to them
Weaknesses	Can lose focus and objectivity if not executed properly
	Does not provide sufficient detail for effective, short-term action
Bottom-Up Planning	
Attributes	Employs an incremental, step-by-step approach
	Based on current conditions
Strengths	Lends itself to immediate evaluation of effectiveness
	Consistent with conventional engineering design methodology
Weaknesses	Tends to focus on short-term problems
	Produces ever-decreasing incremental improvements
	Locks in current technology and structure

shown in Table 3–2. Stahl and Grigsby (1992) note that more and more companies worldwide are competing with strategies based on quality. This competition indicates the seriousness of quality planning—it is central to, and necessary for, long-term survival.

These characteristics describe dynamic quality planning. If you have a planning method with these properties, then you are using DQP. Otherwise, you are not. But the properties are not elements of DQP, or objectives, or things you do. They are simply descriptive. In the next paragraph we will discuss what goes into a dynamic quality planning process, and then we will get into how DQP gets implemented into the corporate structure.

ELEMENTS OF DQP

There are some things that you must put into a planning process in order to have DQP, and there is strong consensus on what these things ought to be.[2] The essential components are listed in Table 3–3 and discussed in detail in subsequent paragraphs.

T A B L E   3–2

Properties of Dynamic Quality Planning

Time horizon	The plan extends beyond the period of performance to include both the duration of activity and the time needed to observe results.
Hierarchy	The major goals are supported by a hierarchy of lower-level goals whose attainment leads to the next higher level goals.
Infrastructure	An effective plan requires an organizational hierarchy integrated horizontally as well as vertically. In this way, quality processes can be deployed across functions with no loss in ownership.
Formal methodology	Systems and resource allocations are formalized and systematic, to achieve stability of processes.
Decisions	An effective plan requires a pattern of decisions, often serial and dependent, and adapted to uncertain outcomes.
Control	The plan has a control process for data collection and analysis, metrics for measurement of progress, and feedback for tracking and improvement.

Committees

The same kind of forums that enhance dynamic thinking can do the same for dynamic planning. Only the objective changes; dynamic planning can profit by free-ranging ideas, oriented to some specific goal. Goals suggest an ordering process, and this is achieved through some logical structure of forums.

Juran (1992) states that an executive-level quality council is fundamental to the success of quality planning. Strategy is the purview of executive management, and without participation at this level quality will not happen. On the other hand, quality by mandate is not usually successful either, so that lower-level quality committees may be necessary also. In these committees all employees participate, and communication is open between all the various committees. In the previous chapter, we pointed out that a common thread between committees can be established by using members of a higher-level committee as chairmen of lower-level committees. An appropriate number of committees depends upon the size of the company, the variety of its functions, and its geographical deployment.

T A B L E 3–3

Elements of Dynamic Quality Planning

Committee(s)	An executive quality council consisting of senior level management provides policy and goals to the corporate quality program. It may be supported by lower-level quality committees, representing all levels of the company.
Policies	Policies are action statements derived from the corporate mission.
Goals	Goals are the desired, measurable results of policy actions.
Deployment	The deployment of goals identifies resources, responsibilities, integration, and "ownerships" specified for achievement.
Evaluation	Performance evaluation requires identifying what is to be evaluated, the metric, the methodology, and feedback for control and improvement.

In principle, every forum and no forum should be quality forums. Meetings whose objective is quality have no tangible purpose, attract no achievers, and turn out to be much ado about nothing. Conversely, meetings whose objective is some tangible goal, near or far, but that ignore quality, will result in a deteriorating sequence of successes, as the customer turns away. The best example to explain this dichotomy is an all-too-typical corporate structure, that of a Department of Defense contractor, say General Armaments. Once a contract is awarded, two departments of General Armaments take center stage: Production and Quality Assurance. In order to satisfy the contract, the head of Quality Assurance reports directly to the president. On paper, it appears as though the Q.A. chief has considerable influence. In fact, he has little. His people may be tolerated on the production line, but they have no technical expertise, and hence no input. Nor do they have any decision-making authority. The Production Chief rules the production line, and he is, in turn, ruled by the schedule. Production meetings are dominated by the schedule. No one from production attends quality meetings. East is East and West is West.

This is not to say that quality assurance departments are worthless. On the contrary, Juran discusses a quality department of the future that provides quality oversight, while quality control is exercised by the production people themselves. This important subject will be discussed in later chapters. At this point, we emphasize that the purpose of a forum is to achieve a goal, and that the driver is quality.

Policies

A company's philosophy must be articulated in a form that can be implemented. One way of doing so is to express corporate policies as guidelines for action, to which goals can be assigned. Thus we see a chain of translation from philosophy to results, shown in Figure 3–1.

Policies, then, are action statements that reflect corporate philosophy. They may vary from company to company, but Juran lists common policies:

1. Meet the needs of customers.
2. Equal or exceed competitive quality.
3. Achieve improvement annually.
4. Extend quality policies to all areas of the business.

For example, a quality policy might be similar to that expressed by McQuay International Corporation (1995):

> It is the policy of McQuay International to provide its customers with products and services that meet or exceed their expectations in terms of quality, availability, and are competitive in total cost.

Goals

A goal is the desired result of the action expressed by a policy. It is specific and measurable. There may be more than one *end* goal per policy. Generally, there will be many goals, as indicated by Figure 3–1, arrayed in a hierarchy described by Gibson as an *objectives tree*. For our purposes, the term *goal* is interchangeable with the word *objective*. In formulating goals, Gibson proposes the following process:

1. Generalize the implementation of the policy.
2. Develop a descriptive scenario of the present situation.
3. Develop a normative scenario of how the situation ought to be.

F I G U R E   3–1

Transition of Ideas into Action

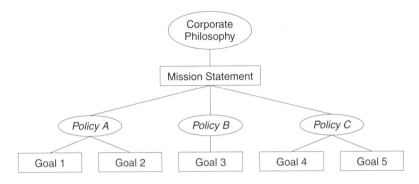

4. Develop the axiological component, that is, the hidden agenda, if any.
5. Prepare an objectives tree.
6. Validate.
7. Iterate.

Determining goals is a top-down activity, so you want to proceed from the general to the specific. The initial cut at creating goals from policy, then, is to start out as general as possible. Don't commit a specific interpretation to a policy right away, because the first idea that comes to mind may not be the best, and may even be wrong. For example, one of the McQuay policies is to differentiate the company from the competition in total cost. One way to do that, for this company, is to go after a very narrow part of the heating, ventilating, and air conditioning (HVAC) market. Or it might instead choose to take the competition head on, across the board. Look at the policy as broadly as possible. Within this broad interpretation, examine how you are now doing things. This is called developing the descriptive scenario.

Once you have established where the company is (what it does; how it does it), then it's time to think about where the company ought to be—the normative scenario. Spend as much time as possible, perhaps in brainstorming, in deciding about this. This process provides direction and will be the springboard for objectives.

The normative scenario describes the way things ought to be, which suggests that values are involved. Not all values are explicit, but values will dominate the direction of the company. Gibson points out that, especially if hidden and stated values conflict, goals may not be achieved. The planners, then, whether they report to high-level management, or whether they themselves are the management, must bring into the open all driving values. For example, some markets may be objectionable to some management, say building strategic missiles, or trading with certain undemocratic nations. These notions reflect controversial values and if they remain hidden, then marketing will be going in one direction and production in another.

An objectives tree is shown in Figure 3–2, and represents a deployment of objectives throughout the organization. Having arrived at a goal that will satisfy corporate policy, all the levels of achievement required to attain the goal are determined, often by brainstorming. As Juran points out, communication *down* the tree tends to impart corporate direction, whereas communication *up* the tree tends to impart cost, because required resources are specified. Certain quality goals tend to be universal: product performance; quality competitiveness; reduction of cost of quality; performance of macroprocesses.

Referring to the McQuay case, the goals are the execution of its policy statement: to meet or exceed customer expectations in quality and availability, and to be competitive in total cost. Then methods must be determined to achieve these goals, and this is done by generating an objectives tree, that is, a set of objectives from the general to the specific, which can be implemented and executed. Goals tend to be *"blue sky,"* that is, "improve profitability." But how can this be done? It is done by determining objectives that are realistic actions that can be taken. One general objective that will improve profitability might be to reduce rework; a specific objective to reduce rework might be to begin statistical process control.

Deployment

The generation of supporting objectives across the functions of the organization creates quality deployment. The detail of how this deployment is achieved will be discussed in a later chapter on

F I G U R E   3–2

An Objectives Tree

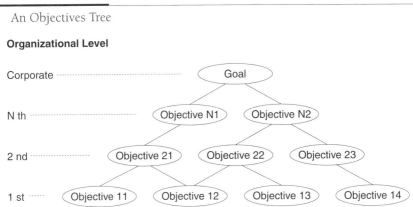

Organizational Level

Corporate .... Goal

N th .... Objective N1   Objective N2

2 nd .... Objective 21   Objective 22   Objective 23

1 st ...... Objective 11   Objective 12   Objective 13   Objective 14

organization. Deployment is a bottom-up activity, which means considerable detail must be provided. It is sufficient here to say that all actions must be functionally integrated, with an "owner" identified for each objective through its life.

Evaluation

Since it takes action to achieve goals, there must be a means of evaluating performance relative to them. The first question is: "What will we measure? What will indicate progress?" The second follows from the first: "What will be the metric?" Sometimes the metric is obvious, sometimes not. For example, if the goal is to increase market share, perhaps the metric might be sales, in dollars. But if, as with McQuay, it is desired to meet or exceed customer expectations in quality and availability, then what do you measure, and what is the metric? The identity of an index of performance must be carefully thought out, avoiding the pitfall of measuring something just because it is easy to measure.

The methodology of measurement must be appropriate also. For stochastic processes, there are numerable statistical methodologies applicable over the life cycle of the process; examples are given in Table 3–4. We will discuss which method is used when in a later chapter, but here we should note that one way or another, they are all concerned with variation of product.

T A B L E   3–4

Statistical Methodologies for System Life Cycle

Life Cycle Phase	Methodology
Design	Process capability analysis
	Analysis of variance (ANOVA)
	Design of experiments
Production	Stability analysis (e.g., control charting)
	On-line process capability measurement
	Fault analysis (e.g., Ishikawa; Pareto)
Near horizon	Reliability analysis
	Maintainability analysis
	Audit

The greatest factor of adversity in production is variance of quality. Design methods are aimed at *prevention* of variance. On-line feedback of key parameters can contribute to design *improvement*. Stability analysis and measurement of process capability during operations are aimed at *detection* of variance. Ishikawa diagrams and Pareto charts are used to *identify* the special causes of variance. Reliability and maintainability measurements are used to determine the effectiveness of design in terms of common causes of variance. Audit is an effective evaluation methodology listed here as a near horizon methodology, but in fact should be used throughout the system life cycle.

IMPLEMENTATION

Summarizing, we find that dynamic quality planning has three characteristics:

1. It includes both top-down and bottom-up planning.
2. It is sensitive to changes in both system *and* environment.
3. It is continuous.

Planning for quality in a dynamic environment is achieved in two simple phases. The first concerns *why*, and is the cerebral sequence of Figure 3–1: philosophy → mission statement → policies

F I G U R E   3–3

A Deming Cycle for Planning

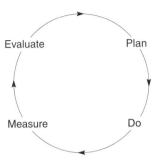

→ goals. The second phase concerns *how,* and is the building of capabilities, processes, and resources to achieve the goals. These phases are neither distinct nor terminal. For example, in the interest of generating unbounded ideas, critique during brainstorming is not permitted, but at some point evaluation of the ideas must take place, and one of the filters is feasibility.

Planning Organization

Similarly, in designing structures to implement the goals, alternative ways to the goals are considered. In some cases either the path to a goal or the goal itself must be rethought. For example, some years ago the management of a weapons system engineering group developed a set of goals to accomplish in an approaching five-year period. One of the goals was to reduce the single-shot probability of kill of a particular missile by 0.5 percent per year. Upon getting into the *how,* they realized that they could measure this probability only to an accuracy of 2 percent. There was no way of determining if any actions taken were causing an improvement or not. Therefore, planning phases must be designed for continual review, forever.

The planning continuum is shown in Figure 3–3 as a Deming, or Shewart, cycle.[3] This very simple drawing is profound in its description of the planning process. There is no delineating point at which one phase begins and another ends, and there is never an end to the planning. Moreover, as Senge et al. (1994) point out, these phases have a cause-and-effect relationship. When the planning structure of a company can be described by this cycle, then planning is properly implemented as a continuum of thinking about an objective, doing something, determining if you're where you ought to be, and then rethinking.

The first step in quality planning is to create the planning forums. The reason for this is that there is a difference between business planning and quality planning. Business planning is usually a line function in an organization, with clear, delineated responsibilities. Quality planning is the integration of the activities of this line function with other functions in the organization that can provide specific expertise to overall planning. This requires forums, and constructive forums require a committee network such as the structures discussed earlier. For example, in planning to develop a new product or to improve an existing one, quality is functionally deployed by a planning committee of marketing, product engineering, manufacturing engineering, production, and purchasing.

These forums are organized to operate within the continuum of Figure 3–3, because they are part of the ongoing planning process. They receive inputs from the evaluation phase. Moreover, the forum membership is fluid. Purchasing may not be brought into a planning activity during the brainstorming period, but should be brought in before any ideas are either thrown out or adopted. The customer is represented at all forums and in all phases, not just by Marketing, but by Field Engineering, Sales, Service, and all line functions that come into contact with him.

Management Responsibility

Quality has all the aspects of a virtue. First, it is in the eye of the beholder, in this case, the customer. Second, it does not just happen, but is the result of a concerted and ongoing effort. Management is responsible for that effort. Quality planning is that planning used to stamp process and product with the virtue of quality, and according to the Deming cycle, is never ending. Furthermore, the implementation must embrace the customer. This concept is shown in Figure 3–4 in terms of direction, organization, and work-

F I G U R E   3–4

Implementing Quality: The Management Responsibility

ing system in mutual support. The simple directive below is a more emphatic statement of this quality responsibility:

Say what you do; do what you say; prove it.

Mike Bradley (1994) uses this maxim to summarize the requirements of the ISO 9000 quality standard, but the Malcolm Baldrige quality standard is no less demanding. If you can't document your quality to the Baldrige auditors, you get a rating called, politely, "anecdotal." The first part of the maxim means that each company is free to set up its own quality system, compatible with its own production processes and way of doing business. However, you must document the system in order to prove that what you do is what you say you do. This paper trail is an absolute requirement of a serious quality plan.

In sum, management must plan to incorporate these responsibilities into its quality system:

1. Define a quality policy and resultant objectives.
2. Ensure corporate commitment at all levels to the quality goals.
3. Deploy and utilize personnel and resources to achieve the goals.

FIGURE 3–5

A Structural Element of a Quality System

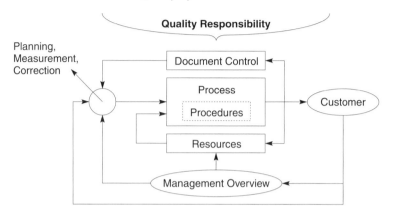

4. Establish a quality representative with appropriate authority and accountability to monitor the quality system.
5. Maintain management review of the quality dynamics.

Quality System

A dynamic quality plan is not implemented unless it is systematic. This quality system is formal. This means that it must be defined by a written, dynamic plan; therefore, it is a living document. As a plan, it describes in detail the who, what, when, where, and why of the corporate quality dynamic. The elements of this dynamic system are repeated here: The organizational structure, responsibilities, procedures, processes, and resources for implementing quality management.

A quality system, as any system, is cybernetic, with many interactive elements. A company is organized functionally in order to generate products and services, but as Juran is fond of pointing out, the functional organization does not ensure synergistic operations. Therefore, a good quality system will integrate functions and operations. An example of this idea is shown in Figure 3–5, which portrays a simple structural element of a quality system.

This structure uses a feedback loop to ensure tracking and improvement. Dynamic quality planning must be systematic, that is, put in the form of a Deming cycle. How do you ensure that the loop is closed? This is achieved through robust design, the subject of the next chapter.

NOTES

1. **Tactical Planning.** Abell (1993) discusses both strategic and tactical planning, but believes that the latter is more effective because it involves the company's workers, those who are experts in its processes. Hewitt (1994) seconds the motion, in a sense, claiming that top management don't usually get involved in tactical planning, nor do they think in terms of variance and its causes. The implication of this is that if there is no employee empowerment, and if top management neglect tactical planning, then their strategic planning is "blue sky" and cannot be effectively implemented.

2. **Elements of DQP.** Stahl and Grigsby (1992), Juran (1992), Abell (1993), and Cuppello (1994) all use similar elements in presenting arguments for dynamism in planning. They do not use the term "dynamic quality planning" per se.

3. **The Deming Cycle.** The Deming Cycle of Plan, Do, Observe, Study was the creation of Walter A. Shewart, and Deming himself always referred to it as the Shewart Cycle. In his book *Out of the Crisis*, Deming relates that it began to be called the Deming Cycle in Japan, and now that term is in general use. The cycle used in Chapter 3 is modified somewhat to suit the purposes at hand. In principle, it is nevertheless a Deming cycle.

REFERENCES

Abell, Derek F. *Managing with Dual Strategies*. New York: Free Press, MacMillan Inc., 1993.

Bradley, Michael. *ISO 9000 for the Global Market*. Videotape of Perry Johnson, Inc., 1994.

Collins, James C., and Jerry I. Porras. *Built to Last: Successful Habits of Visionary Companies*. New York: Harper Business, 1994.

Comdial Corporation. *Mission Statement*. Charlottesville, VA: Comdial Corp., 1995.

Cupello, James M. "A New Paradigm for Measuring TQM Progress." *Quality Progress*, May 1994, pp. 79–82.

Gibson, John E. *How to Do Systems Analysis.* Englewood Cliffs, NJ: Prentice Hall (in review).

Goldratt, Eliyahu M., and Jeff Cox. *The Goal: A Process of Continuous Improvement.* New York: North River Press, 1986.

Hayes, Robert H., and Steven C. Wheelwright. *Restoring Our Competitive Edge: Competing through Manufacturing.* New York: Copyright © 1984 John Wiley. Reprinted by permission of John Wiley & Sons, Inc.

Hewitt, Steven. "Strategic Advantages Emerge from Tactical Tools." *Quality Progress,* October 1994, pp. 57–59.

Juran, Joseph M. *Juran on Quality by Design.* New York: Copyright © 1992 by Juran Institute, Inc. Published by the Free Press, an imprint of Simon & Schuster.

McQuay International. *Quality Policy.* Minneapolis: McQuay World Headquarters, 1995.

Metro Machine Corporation. *Quality Policy.* Norfolk, VA: Metro Machine Corp., 1994.

Senge, Peter; Charlotte Roberts; Richard Ross; Bryan J. Smith; and Art Kleiner. *The Fifth Discipline Fieldbook.* New York: Doubleday, 1994.

Stahl, Michael J., and David W. Grigsby. *Strategic Management for Decision Making.* Boston: Copyright © 1992. PWS-Kent Publishing. Reproduced with the permission of Southwestern College Publishing, a division of International Thomson Publishing Inc. All rights reserved.

Tomasko, Robert M. *Rethinking the Corporation.* New York: Copyright © 1993. Reprinted with permission of the publisher, AMACOM, a division of the American Management Association.

4

⑥ DESIGNING ROBUST PROCESSES

THE PROCESS OF DESIGN

> It is a generally accepted fact that the correct formulation of a problem takes roughly 50 percent of the total effort needed to solve it.
>
> *Jasbir Arora, 1989*

Most of us have designed something—a building, a cake, or a garden—and get a great deal of fun out of it because our artistic nature gets to take over. This kind of designing is important, and whether at home or in industry, satisfies our intuitive notion of what designing means. But given that you have designed something, say a product, if you want to reproduce it infinitely many times, then you need also to design a production process that can do it, and you need a robust design process to do *that*.

This argument is not limited to products. Suppose that you want to provide a high-quality service repeatedly, then you need to design the process that can do it. This is true whether your service is provided to an external or to an internal customer. An external customer is one we normally think of as a customer, a person outside the company. An internal customer is one inside the company, for example, an accounting department. This means that organizational processes must be designed, too. All robust processes, organizational or productive, must be designed to be robust. Robustness doesn't happen on its own.

For example, Kramer (1993) discusses the geographic design needed to compete globally. Given this objective, you want to come up with an effective organization. By correctly formulating the organizational design, you can maximize your proximity to foreign markets while minimizing duplication of functions. This amounts to making arrangements of system elements within a grand structure and is in no way different from arranging system elements within a factory or on a breadboard.

MacKenzie's study (1986) of line organizations found that the correspondence between how they appear on paper and how they really operate was, for most companies, less than 50 percent, and that a good one would rate about 60 percent. This happens because the designers failed to realize that organizational design must be formulated just as production processes are. A process is a process. If we call activities by their functional name—human or machine—then we can get past our prejudices, for optimum design methods can be used to achieve robustness for any process. Let's talk about the design process itself—how to design productive *and* organizational systems.

Back in Chapter 1 we said that design and planning were similar. Of course, they are listed as synonyms in the thesaurus, but from an engineering point of view we want to ensure that the design and planning *processes* are similar. For if they are, and if a robust design process exists, then by extension, a robust planning process can be found. From there it follows that a robust organization can be created using engineering techniques.

The design process begins with a set of customer requirements, as shown in Figure 4–1. Specifications are determined that will meet the requirements, then modeling begins. The modeling consists of various stages of design, until a prototype is reached. Modeling is the essence of design—we never create something from nothing—but let's postpone a discussion on modeling for another chapter because there is much to say about it. Figure 4–1 is an extremely general description of the design process in any field: hardware engineering, software engineering, operations research, ship design, and so on. The term *waterfall* comes from the software world, but the process is nonetheless universal. The feature that might vary from one application to another is the feedback structure.

FIGURE 4-1

The Waterfall Model of a System Design Process

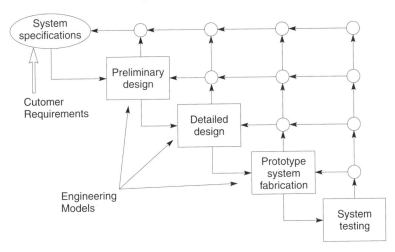

The feedback loops in the design process allow for verification, validation, and correction at each step of the way. At any stage, you can send the design back to an earlier stage, or even go back and change the specifications if it appears necessary. For example, a particular thickness of laminated wood may be called for in the "specs," but as the design develops and costs are analyzed, it may be found feasible to make the wood thinner, or necessary to make it even thicker or to replace the wood with metal because of conflicting thickness and weight constraints. Since feedback represents an activity, it is not free. The simpler the product, the simpler the process may be to produce it. A large software program, a spreadsheet, for example, or hardware system such as a telecommunications system, will require feedback loops throughout the process.

Although the waterfall is a general design process, many software engineers reject it because there is no working software until late in the game, which impedes reliability estimation. They prefer a spiral, or rapid prototyping process as shown in Figure 4–2. Again, this is a somewhat general design process because something like it is used in some hardware engineering. Although hardware construction can be expensive, so that a single prototype is

FIGURE   4-2

The Spiral Design, or Rapid Prototyping Process

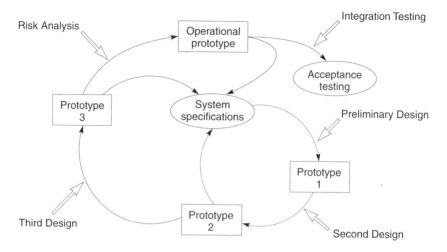

the usual case, upgrades to the prototype may be cost-feasible. The essence of rapid prototyping is the access back to specifications, if necessary, for each iteration of design based upon prototype results. The key issue here is that just as design calls for imagination, so does the design of the process to be used to effect the product design. You adapt a design process to meet your needs. It must be disciplined, that is, well defined, in order to get repeatability. You need constraints on the system, but not on your mind.

The two basic design processes discussed thus far can be varied to satisfy almost any process design requirement. A major variant is called optimum design, which we'll discuss in the next chapter on modeling. Rupp and Russell (1994) point out, however, that there are several unique characteristics to *redesign* that must be added to any general design process. Most important of these is to answer the question: why do you want to change the system? Answering this question identifies the problem, and sets up two parallel channels in the subsequent design process. The first is the process restructuring path, which can be either of the two general processes or their variants. The second is the problem-solving path, which is necessary to ensure that the redesign satisfies its objective.

GOALS AND FUNCTIONS

It takes action to achieve an objective, and it takes a system of actions to achieve a set of objectives. Most people have a good intuitive grasp of what a system is, something like Gibson's definition (1990): *"A system is a set of elements so interconnected as to aid in driving toward a defined goal."* You can understand *system* with this definition, but you can't build one with it. You need to know that the rigor in making interconnections effective is very specific, and the word *element* is very general. We will define a system element as an assigned activity, that is, a function.[1] Then a more specific definition of *system* is a set of elements consisting of a performance function, **S**, a controller function, **C**, and an integrating function, $\int$, which, when subject to a permissible driving function, **F**, and a defined event set, **E**, result in a state, **X**, whose trajectory leads to the attainment of the system objective.[2] Properly integrated, a collection of systems so defined comprises a larger system and leads to the attainment of a prescribed goal.

This larger system is portrayed in Figure 4–3. There are **n** subsystems comprising the system shown in this figure, but for brevity only the first and last are indicated. The components of the subsystems are often delineated by a subscript such as S_1 or C_n. The three dots separating them indicate that there are other subsystems in parallel between them. The component S_1 in the figure is a performance function designed to achieve an objective. The controller function C_1 keeps its state trajectory on track. The integrating function $\int$ integrates the **n** processes to achieve both their objectives and the system goal. It should be borne in mind that a function is executed by a human, a machine, or both. For example, a controller may be a gear assembly, a computer, or a supervisor. The dynamic speed may differ depending upon the nature of the controller, but the dynamic form does not. The symbol $F_n(E,t)$ refers to the driving force acting upon the nth subsystem. It is a subset of events from the event set E, arriving at some time, t. For example, if the process of Figure 4–3 depicted a project, then the set of events would be the work package, where different groups of the work items within that package would be acted upon by the various subprocesses composing the system.

F I G U R E   4–3

Achieving Objectives through Functions

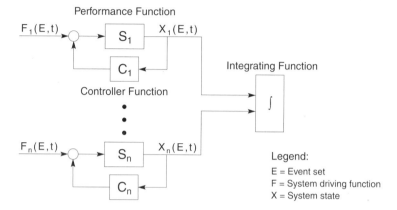

Figure 4–4 depicts an example of an integrated system. A ship repair yard wants to effect a major ship alteration, or Ship Alt, in the vernacular. A number of shops are needed to achieve this goal as many varied tasks must be accomplished. Although the hierarchy of a shipyard is vertical, Juran (1992) points out that things get done horizontally. Thus, extra effort and organization are required in order to avoid interference and to promote efficiency. Work must be coordinated both in planning and in execution. In this case, the integration is achieved through coordination. Shop supervisors are in constant communication with each other, as well as with their workers. This communication provides the system feedback. Ownership of the ship alteration belongs to the ship supervisor.

ATTRIBUTES AND CONTROLS

In order for the function group of performer, controller, and integrator to be effective, certain attributes and controls must obtain. Each group must have the attributes of *stability, capability,* and *improvability.* And each group must have three controls: *responsibility, authority,* and *accountability.* We usually ascribe the terms *responsibility, authority,* and *accountability* to humans, but they are in any case good words to describe controlling action. It is important

FIGURE 4-4

A Ship Repair Yard Integrates Its Shop Activities to Achieve a Major Goal: Ship Alt 253K

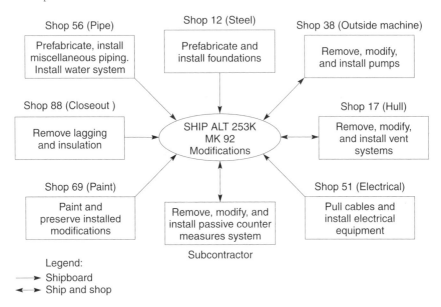

in systems design to keep things general as long as possible. This prevents arriving at fixed ideas before it is time to fix them. So without regard to the nature of a particular function, we want to think about the attributes and the controls that we want to design into it. For example, it must be stable and it must have the authority to do its job. When you think about it, this sentence makes sense whether we are talking about an assembly line worker or a printed circuit card.

There is another important benefit to using attributes and controls in a general sense. When a process has humans in the loop, they are part of the system. They always have an assigned responsibility, but do not always have authority or accountability, as outside auditors often discover. By designing a system with these controls in place, it is easier to talk about the lack of authority or accountability because it is depersonalized and can be discussed in systems engineering terms.

Stability[3]

A process is stable in the sense of Lyapunov if its state trajectory remains bounded for a bounded input (driving function). A process is stable in the sense of Shewart if its product variability is bounded. Usually, this means that the product variation is within 3σ (99.73 percent) limits of a mean or standard value. Thus, whether a process is dynamic or stochastic, the property of stability is a defined requirement.

Capability

A process is capable in a stochastic sense if its product variability is bounded within specifications. Usually, this means that the product variation is within specification limits. Notice that a process can be stable and not be capable. The variability of the process may well be bounded, but if that variability exceeds the specification, then the process is not capable. You need to design a new process. A process must be stable before its capability can be determined.

Improvability

A process is improvable in the sense of Taguchi if incremental product variation is measured and can be reduced. For example, a product with hard upper and lower limits is not improvable because as long as degradation is within the limits it is not measured. A process is improvable in the sense of Deming if its customer appeal can be increased. This idea is realized in Figure 4–5. The customer-driven feedback ensures that the process tracks customer satisfaction and brings about improvement as customer requirements dictate. It is worth noting that Figure 4–5 can be considered a "superstructure," or overview, of Figure 4–3.

Responsibility

Control is achieved through responsibility by precisely defining and assigning the task and metric of the performance function. Metric refers to the index of performance used to measure the achievement of quality in the task. Whether the function is performed by a human or a machine, *responsibility* aptly describes the

FIGURE   4–5

A Continuous Improvement Mechanism to Improve Quality

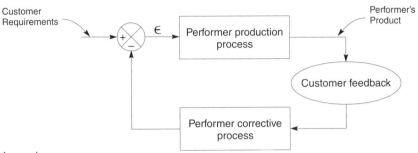

Legend:
$\in$ = customer requirements less producer's product
$\in$ = 0 means customer satisfaction

execution and measurement of the function, and thus is used here in a very general sense. It may sound strange to say "this machine's responsibility," but generalizing our thoughts frees us from preconceived limitations about people and machines.

Authority

Control is achieved through authority by the availability and provision of the resources required to achieve the task. This includes human, material, and capital resources, as well as time. Whether the function is performed by a human or a machine, *authority* aptly describes the range and power available to the function, and thus is used here in a very general sense. For example, suppose that a computer-controlled machine is installing two-lead components on a printed circuit card, and runs out of feeder tape. You wouldn't say that the machine no longer has authority—that would sound awkward, to say the least. You would simply say what you have always said: the machine is out of tape. But, to be consistent about it, neither would you say that a project manager has run out of authority. You *would* say that he never had proper authority to begin with. And so you might say of a machine, and still make sense. In designing a system, do not think in terms of a person or a machine. Think in terms of function and control.

Accountability

Control is achieved through accountability by imposing a penalty function for off-target performance. *Penalty* has a negative connotation here. One must account for failure to achieve or maintain the task optimally. Thus, accountability is the control used to attain the attribute of improvability. The penalty function is usually nonlinear, imposing a greater penalty in proportion to the deviation from target objective. Whether the function is performed by a human or a machine, *accountability* aptly describes the sensitivity and liability of the function, and thus is used here in a very general sense.

Penalty function is also called *cost function,* to escape the negative connotation of the word *penalty.* In the next chapter, we will show that a process may be designed with an inherent penalty function. For example, the speed of an automatic lathe is controlled by a number of weighted factors; as the lathe becomes dull, the lathe will increase speed in compensation. The penalty, as it were, is the increased cost in running the lathe at a higher speed. Similarly, if a project falls behind schedule, the project manager may call for the expenditure of more man-hours. Penalty, then, refers to the additional cost of compensation.

One might argue that the terms *responsibility* and *accountability* are redundant. This may be true in the dictionary, but usually not the case in industry and government. In modern organizational usage, responsibility has come to refer to the assignment of a function or task. The task may not always be achieved. For example, a production manager may be responsible for both schedule and quality control, but only accountable for schedule. If the schedule slips to the point where the time for acceptance testing is impacted, the supervisor will often not hesitate to abandon the testing. Accountability means that the task *must* be achieved or a penalty is paid.

In our example, testing is abandoned in order to avoid a late delivery, which carries with it a certain cost of quality, say customer dissatisfaction. But if a faulty part is delivered to the customer, the company will pay a much higher cost of quality than might have been the case if testing had taken place and the fault located in the shop. In this case, the company itself is held accountable by the

F I G U R E   4–6

The Design Control Process

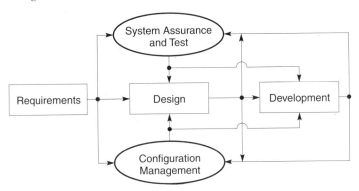

customer. Since the production supervisor was not accountable for testing, the playing field of production and test was not level. Lack of accountability favors short-term over long-term penalties, even though the latter almost certainly will be greater. This adds a distorted and invisible element in the decision-making process.

DESIGN CONTROL

Design control has to do with the operations of design and development planning, design input and output, verification and validation, and design changes. As Lamprecht (1993) points out, design is a multiparty activity, involving suppliers and external customers in addition to the many internal customers. Things can quickly get away from you as players go off each group on its own tangent. One way to keep everyone aware of progress and of what has been accepted or rejected is to formalize cohesiveness through group sessions and documentation. As Figure 4–6 shows, configuration management is an important part of the process. In the early stages of design, in particular, when requirements may be fuzzy and alternatives many, document control can be undisciplined. Ideas are tried and abandoned. Without a paper trail it may be difficult to review why some design changes were made and others rejected.

Both verification and validation are part of the design control. They are commonly distinguished by two simple questions, put by Boehm (1984):

Verification answers the question: "Are we doing things right?"

Validation answers the question: "Are we doing the right things?"

Validation will certainly occur in contract review, but in the design of complex systems this important step should be taken at each phase of the design process. The same is true of verification, which will also continue through system testing and delivery. There are commonly recognized procedures for validation and verification:

1. Hold design reviews.
2. Conduct feasibility tests and demonstrations.
3. Determine alternative calculations.
4. Compare the new design with a similar proven design, if available.

Some of these suggestions have already been made, but are repeated here to show the universality of them. The last suggestion is a type of benchmarking, and is always done. If the performance of your prototype is in the ballpark of a related product, this lends credibility to any improvement that it displays.

IMPLEMENTATION

It is difficult enough to effect a good design from well-defined requirements. In practice, however, customer requirements are often indirect or assumed. This is why you begin every design as you begin every plan—generalize the problem or the perceived requirement. You think about how the existing product or service works, and using brainstorming techniques, arrive at some ideas for improvement. These ideas must be translated into at least tentative specifications, because design is an art of implementation and you have to design to real numbers. For example, it may be perceived in the airline industry that the customer wants to go faster. You can't design "faster." This requirement must be translated into specifications that you can aim for in your design. This leads to a feasibility study of alternatives, until a best option is determined and a preliminary design is arrived at. The preliminary design is equivalent to the normative scenario that we talked about in planning. In our example of fast air transport, the options might be faster airplanes, more direct routes, fewer exchanges, faster baggage handling, and so on. In other words, "faster" can be interpreted as speed from terminal to terminal, or from home to destination. The latter definition opens up many more alternatives.

A set of alternatives derived from brainstorming will include several feasible ones, among which there may be no optimum. You look at the advantages and disadvantages of each, and find that trade-offs are quite ambiguous. If that is the case, give greater weight to the alternative with the most simple structure. In organization, simplicity is a virtue.

Tomasko (1993) suggests a horizontal structure to the design, but this advice needs to be implemented with care. Horizontal structures require quality deployment if the process interfaces outside its own unit. Quality deployment is not technically hard, but it is socially difficult. You achieve it through the concept of *ownership*. An *owner* is a person that controls the process or process interfaces throughout its passage from one unit to another, until a new owner is assigned. And control here means responsibility, authority, and accountability. Suppose that we have a product, say an important document, passing from purchasing to production. While the document is in purchasing, purchasing owns it. When in production, production owns it. But who owns it in transit? It is precisely the managerially ambiguous area between line functions in which so much responsibility is lost.

Some years ago, during a missile exercise on the Pacific Missile Range, the detection suite of a U.S. Navy destroyer had detected a threat and established track on it. The track was then passed over to the ship's missile system for engagement, except that the engagement suite couldn't find it. Radar maintenance men insisted that nothing was wrong with their detection systems. Operations systems guys insisted just as emphatically that their systems were working fine. And, of course, the fire control technicians said: "Hey, our systems passed daily testing this morning; you're sending us a bad track." I tell this story because missile exercises are terribly exciting, and because this chain of events goes on all the time in multifunctional businesses. If a product passes through organizational lines, there must be an owner.

The owner doesn't have to be a human being. In the case of the destroyer, *integrated* testing that morning would have revealed the inability of one system, performing correctly in its own modes, to interface properly with another system. This is what is meant by the integration block shown in Figure 4–3. We would assume that processes that are subsystems of a larger system would be fully integrated. Sometimes they are, but even in those cases, full integration may be taken off-line so that subsystems can be used independently. And, of course, if the interfacing processes are departments within an organization, there may be no integration. Ownership provides this necessary function.

Both the design of a process and the process itself will require decision making. Ackoff et al. (1984) provide some good ideas in designing decision making into the process. Decision making should be assigned at the lowest level at which information is available. All those who are affected by a decision should have some say in it. And measures of performance of employees should be developed collaboratively with them. These are quality issues, and Deming would agree with them. But let's be politically incorrect here. Employee empowerment, a big issue today, is about decision making. We talked in an earlier chapter about the axiological component in value systems and decision making. There is always privileged information. Many companies will not let employees or lower-level management spend the company's money. Sometimes there simply is no money in the bank, an admission that few CEOs are likely to share with employees. Few people within a company have the authority to change an existing contract, and some on-line decisions will do just that, so here again, there must be limits on empowerment.

Generally, subordinates are reasonable about the right to make decisions. It's not just the right to make decisions on issues that concern them; many companies already provide that right. It has to do with decisions about how and when a job will be done. You get responsible behavior from employees when you give them responsibility. Giving decision-making authority to employees is placing maximum trust in them, and is good quality policy. If there are decisions about how the job should be done that cannot be delegated, then explaining why not is a reasonable thing to do, and will be accepted reasonably.

There are, finally, certain characteristics that should be in every design. MacKenzie (1986) lists a dozen of them as desiderata; two are repeated here as particularly good ideas. Given any two alternative designs, the one that is most specific about details and assumptions is preferred. And the organizational design should leave provision for maintenance and updating. The reasoning for both should be apparent. A design that is vague in detail or that is based upon vague (or false) assumptions cannot be made robust, because metrics and triggers cannot respond to vague parameters. Provisions for maintenance and updating allow for improvability. Interestingly, this sounds like motherhood—who doesn't agree? And yet, we see systems that cannot be maintained except with great difficulty, and if you want proof, simply look under the hood of your car.

We've talked about the process of design. In the next chapter, we will discuss how you design processes: dynamic, stochastic, continuous, discrete event—in short, modeling. The models will be kept brief and general for two reasons. First, in order to completely design a model, you need great detail, a book full, and there are many books available. Second, we want to use these models to achieve robust processes in organizations, which often have multiple missions, and great flexibility is required.

NOTES

1. **Function.** In general usage, a function is the proper action of an agent. If we regard the agent as the independent variable, then the function is dependent upon the agent. From this point of view, the mathematical definition of *function* agrees with general usage, and the term is appropriate to use in the description of a system. Within the context of a system, the activity related to the function is very general. It can be management, electrical filtering, analysis, water sluicing, banking, mechanical assembly, and so on.

2. **System.** Kalman et al. (1969) have defined a deterministic system rigorously as an abstract mathematical concept composed of the following axiomatic vector spaces: an admissible input, single-valued output functions, all possible states, and a state transition function. If the system is stochastic, then a space of events must also be included,

with associated probabilities. The Kalman definition is often used in design, but is difficult for nonengineers to understand. The definition of a system that is offered for use in this book is a compromise between the easy-to-understand intuitive definition, which is too ambiguous to be used for design purposes, and the hard-to-understand Kalman definition. Another point that must be made concerns the "larger system" of Figure 4–3, in which the systems may be regarded as subsystems. This concept is acceptable within the definition of the word, and is in agreement with general usage. For example, the solar system can be considered as a subsystem of the universe, and as an element of the infinite cosmos. However, it is not quite all a matter of perspective. Once a system has been defined, everything beyond the system is regarded as its environment, which is dealt with in a different way. Finally, the definition of system also applies to process. We will not distinguish between *process* and *system* in this book.

3. **Stability**. This subject is discussed at some length in Chapter 5, on process dynamics, but two important names in stability have been raised here, and their introduction is appropriate. M. A. Lyapunov is considered the father of stability theory, and presented his classical work in Paris in 1893. Briefly, according to Lyapunov, dynamic systems are stable if they have stable equilibrium states. Shewart also enjoys the prestige of being the father of control charting. Again, briefly, according to Shewart, stochastic systems are stable if they have a stable distribution.

REFERENCES

Ackoff, Russell L.; Jamshid Gharajedaghi; and Elsa Vergara Finnel. *A Guide to Controlling Your Corporation's Future*. New York: John Wiley & Sons, 1984.

Arora, Jasbir S. *Introduction to Optimum Design*. New York: McGraw-Hill, 1989.

Boehm, Barry W. "Verifying and Validating Software Requirements and Design Specifications." *IEEE Transactions, Software Engineering*, January 1984, pp. 75–80.

Gibson, John E. *How to Do Systems Analysis*. Englewood Cliffs, NJ: Prentice Hall (in review).

Juran, Joseph M. *Juran on Quality by Design*. New York: Copyright © 1992 by Juran Institute, Inc. Published by the Free Press, an imprint of Simon & Schuster.

Kalman, R. E.; R. L. Falb; and M. A. Arbib. *Topics in Mathematical System Theory*. New York: McGraw Hill Book Company, 1969.

Kramer, Robert J. *Organizing for Global Competitiveness: The Geographic Design*. New York: The Conference Board, Inc., 1993.

Lamprecht, James L. *Implementing the ISO 9000 Series*. New York: Marcel Dekker, Inc., 1993. Reprinted by courtesy of Marcel Dekker, Inc.

MacKenzie, Kenneth D. *Organizational Design: The Organizational Audit and Analysis Technology*. Norwood, NJ: Ablex Publishing Corp., 1986.

Rupp, Roger O., and James R. Russell. "The Golden Rules of Process Redesign." *Quality Progress*, December 1994, pp. 85–90.

Tomasko, Robert M. *Rethinking the Corporation*. New York: Copyright © 1993. Reprinted with permission of the publisher, AMACOM, a division of the American Management Association.

5

⑥ PROCESS DYNAMICS

A NOTION OF STABILITY

Stability is an essential property of motion . . . It is important to note that stability analysis of motions can be reduced to a stability analysis of the equilibrium state.

Dragoslav Šiljak, 1969

Stability is central to dynamic systems. Although engineers spend a great deal of time considering this property, a notion of stability should be appreciated by business managers who are concerned with managing a dynamic process within a dynamic environment. In Chapter 4 we introduced this idea very briefly in terms of both deterministic and stochastic systems. In this chapter we shall discuss what these things mean in order to arrive at an understanding of how stability affects our business operations.

A deterministic process is one that behaves in a predictable way when disturbed by a known input. A deterministic industrial process is stable if the set of states that it goes to or through (called the state trajectory) remains bounded when disturbed by a bounded input. A state describes what a process is doing, so that a sequence of changes of state describes the "behavior" of the process. The stability of a process thus has the same connotation as, say, the stability of a person.

A bounded input is simply one that begins and ends. A finite number of purchase orders are a bounded input. A workers' strike of 20 days is a bounded input. A fire that cannot be put out and destroys the plant is an unbounded input. A workers' strike of three years, although strictly speaking finite, can be considered an unbounded input because its length is so much greater than any production cycle that the result is calamitous, effectively out of control.

A stochastic process is one that behaves in a random way when disturbed by a known input. Now *randomness* includes not just mildly unpredictable outcomes, but can suggest outcomes that are so totally unpredictable that we have no idea about the outcome—chaos, if you will. In fact, few random processes behave that way; most have behavior whose form is known—it's just that we can't predict exact states or outcomes. Although randomness may be caused by events, it can often be indexed to time. Purchased parts may not arrive on schedule but may arrive randomly a few days early or late. We record the date of their arrival, thus indexing the randomness to time. A stochastic process is simply a random process indexed to time, as are most business and industrial processes. For this reason, I prefer to use the term *stochastic* process rather than random process. The behavior of a stochastic process, when subject to a disturbance, can be understood in general form even though its future states cannot be predicted exactly.

A stochastic industrial process is stable if it manufactures product whose quality variation has a distribution with constant mean and variance over time. These intuitive notions of stability are sufficient for our purposes. They hold irrespective of the size or nature of the system: industrial, business, social, or whatever. For example, a stochastic monetary process is stable if its fluctuation in the money market has a constant mean and variance over time. (By this definition, inflation is a destabilizer. Surprised?) A stochastic delivery service is stable under the same definition. This does not mean that Federal Express, for example, must deliver every package on time. It does mean that if the variation and average of Federal Express's deliveries are bounded, then their service is stable. Is it satisfactory? That's another question to be dealt with elsewhere. At this point, we realize that understanding stability and being able to measure it enhance our ability to manage a dynamic organization.

Šiljak's penetrating observation must be taken in the broadest view. Motion, in this context, does not refer to a transition from one geographical point to another, but is much more general. It refers to a transition from one system state to another. Any dynamic body has states, and some of them are in equilibrium. Once there, the system tends to stay there. This idea applies to industrial states, also.

We are concerned with how a process changes and how it might be controlled in order to maintain or improve quality characteristics. In order to do that, we must consider the states of the process, for this is what changes. The idea is to define a set of useful quality states with equilibrium points within that set. We shall call that set of states a *state space* because the set figuratively generates a space that can be envisioned in our minds, at least for the case where there are only two or three dimensions. Lest you think this is irrelevant, consider that companies spend millions of dollars to forecast markets, and that the ability to imagine or *see* the possible future values of a market is important to understanding its variability. The set of all those values, over time, constitutes a sort of forecast space.

An equilibrium point is a point at which a body is in balance. It doesn't have to be still. Baryshnikov could leap through the air, twist about in space, and land facing the direction whence he leapt, landing absolutely in balance. Jean Claude Killy, the Olympic skiing champion, claimed always to be in balance so long as his feet were beneath him. An equilibrium state is one that is in balance. This idea is demonstrated in Figure 5–1, by showing a child's toy, a top, in two different positions, both in equilibrium. However, top (a) can be maintained in equilibrium only by keeping it spinning.

So too, a business activity can have equilibrium states, some stable, some not. Consider a maker of fabric. Suppose that the selling price is very good, say he earns a profit of 15 percent on the top of the line. However, his process is unknowingly not in control and he has a secondary market of rags. The Operations Boss claims a constant production rate—no problem. Thus, the manufacturer has a process in equilibrium, but if the waste is large enough he's going out of business.

The recognition of equilibrium states and their stability is basic to effective management. If we define a set of possible states

FIGURE 5–1

A Top in Equilibrium: (a) Unstable; (b) Stable

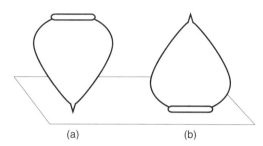

(a) (b)

for our business, and that set has no equilibrium points, then we have chosen an unworkable state space. If there are, then we may be able to achieve a dynamically stable equilibrium state, although the cost of stability must be considered. The basis of this achievement lies in the notion of *controllability*. A system is *controllable* if it can be taken from any given state to any desired state in finite time. Obviously, we want to design a controllable system. In this chapter we will discuss the concept of state and different kinds of processes and the models that might be associated with them, because we design from models. By understanding dynamic models we reinforce our knowledge from the previous chapter on design analysis.

THE QUALITY STATE

What is the state of a system? We often equate *state* with *condition,* as in, "I was in a terrible state." But we cannot afford this redundancy because in business, as well as in science, both state and condition are important enough to be treated distinctly. Intuitively, we say that the state of a system refers to what it is *doing*. More formally, the state of a system is an internal attribute at the present moment that determines the present output and affects future outputs. As an example, the state of an inventory might be the count of a given item. The state of a fast food restaurant might be the number of people in queue. The state of a branch bank might be the amount in outstanding loans. Notice that in all these cases, the state is a variable and there is nothing unique about it. We can

F I G U R E   5–2

A Representation of a Three-Dimensional State Space

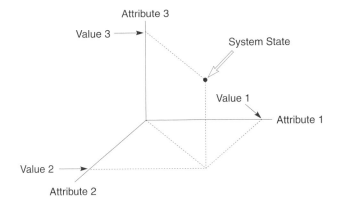

take any attribute of the system that we wish and declare it the state. The only restriction in our selection is that the attribute must be meaningful dynamically and with respect to quality. The first obtains if the selected attribute determines present outputs and affects future outputs of the system. The second obtains if the attribute reflects a quality characteristic. For example, long queues lead to customer dissatisfaction, so that queue length can be chosen as a quality state for fast food restaurants.

We may decide that several attributes are needed to portray the state of our system. Each is called, reasonably enough, a state variable. For example, if we provide a delivery service, then one quality attribute might be the percentage of pieces that are lost, and the other might be delivery time. These become our state variables because they describe the state of our quality system. Notice that in this case the state variables do not have the same metric. One is a percentage, the other an integer, say six hours or two days. State variables do not have to be measured in the same units. However, it takes both of them to describe the state of our quality system. Again, we can choose as many state variables as we wish, but in evaluating quality performance, all of them must be considered or we have chosen to measure too many attributes.

Figure 5–2 depicts a state space of three state variables—attributes 1, 2, and 3—which might represent, in our delivery service, the two previous attributes, plus, say, customer complaints per 1,000 pieces. Each attribute represents an axis of state space, and each state variable has a value measured along its corresponding axis. If we have more than three state variables, then we cannot envision the state space, but that does not lessen the utility of the concept. We shall see in later paragraphs that there are techniques to explore a system's state space looking for optimum values, no matter what the number of dimensions of the space.

Federal Express uses a quality index of 12 components that measure the quality of its service (Lovelock, 1990). The measurements of these components are taken daily. The orientation is taken from the customer's viewpoint; one of the components, for example, is the number of customer complaints. In this case, the lower the score, the higher the quality of service. Although not so named, the components of the Federal Express quality index may be regarded as state variables of a quality state space.

The American Management Association (1982) reported that American Express also used a service quality index which, at the time of reporting, contained 180 variables. From a technical point of view, as well as from a management point of view, this is probably too many. In the first case, it's beyond analysis; and in the second, it's beyond control. If you really think that the quality of your product or service is described by 180 attributes, then you probably need to decentralize quality.

The advantage of the state space concept is that, given enough data, a space can be created that has all of the characteristics of geography: highs, lows, saddle points, steep cliffs, and other surface phenomena. How can this be? Well, consider our example of a delivery service where we have identified two state variables: delivery time and number of pieces lost. We want to reduce them both, but intuitively, we recognize that if we reduce delivery time too much, the tactics that achieved this might well increase the number of pieces lost. We might be able to reduce them both for a time, only to find that at some average value of delivery time, the number of pieces lost increases precipitously (a "cliff" in the state topology).

State space can be used to detect trends, help in predictions, and identify equilibrium states. Once the equilibria are known, then management can make knowledgeable decisions about quality improvements. *Product* improvements can bring the system to its optimum equilibrium state, but if that is not satisfactory to the customer, then a *process* improvement is necessary.

DYNAMIC PROCESSES

Processes change either as a function of time or events, or both. By change, we mean that their state changes. This change of state may occur either because of a change in internal conditions, or in the environment, or in the external forces that drive the process. These external forces can be deterministic driving functions such as electrical power, raw materials, or customer requirements. They can also be random perturbations such as inclement weather, change in market demand, or labor strife.

Processes that change as a function of time are called dynamic processes, although many people insist that event-driven processes are dynamic also.[1] This point is not worth arguing about because, invariably, event-driven processes are indexed to time anyway. For example, the stock market is event driven (buying and selling of stock), but is always indexed to time. We shall adopt the convention that a process that can change state is dynamic, no matter what the cause.

Processes can change state either continuously or discretely with time. Discrete time is an ordered sequence of points in time rather than a continuum. Examples of continuous time processes are flight, aging, machining, banking, migration, the economy, and the life of a city. Examples of discrete time processes are a pulse radar tracking system, the digital computer, and the conduct of an experiment or poll by taking samples in increments of time.

Random processes, as we discussed earlier, are those whose future state cannot be exactly predicted, no matter what our present knowledge. They change their state randomly in time, and we cannot know exactly when, or exactly to what state they will go. We have agreed that when the random change in state is indexed to the time that it occurs, it is called a *stochastic process*. Therefore, the stock market is a stochastic process. A project is another. If samples of a stochastic process are taken in equal intervals, the sequence is called a *time series*. A control chart can be considered a time series whether it is a plot of a quality value or of a quality state.

Random processes that change as a function of events are called *discrete event processes,* or more commonly, *discrete event dynamic systems.* Examples are queues, inventory, delivery, and transportation systems. (Transportation systems are not designed to be random; the German railway system of 1914 to 1918 is touted to have worked on schedule. If so, it is the exception that proves the rule.) Projects are not usually thought of as discrete event processes, but they often behave that way. Necessarily, a random event occurs at some time according to the clock. Thus, the event can be indexed to time, so some savants insist that any random process is a stochastic process. We shall adopt this convention, also, and summarize our conventions in this way:

1. If a process can change state, it is dynamic.
2. If a process changes state randomly, it is stochastic.
3. If a process changes state predictably, it is deterministic.

If we reread our descriptions of stability in the opening paragraphs, we see that the stability of processes is manifested in similar ways. The deterministic system has a bounded response to a bounded input. The stochastic system has a bounded variation to a bounded input. We will demonstrate this idea with an example of control charting.

The father of statistical quality control, Walter Shewart, recognized that the measured quality of manufactured product always has a certain amount of variation as a result of chance. He devised control charting to track that variation. Figure 5–3 portrays one type of control chart. The center line represents the average of the daily samples of the quality attribute. The daily samples are themselves averages of the measured value that the process is set up to produce, but which it does with a certain amount of deviation. To simplify things, assume that the deviation is normally distributed, so that 99.73 percent of the product falls within $\pm 3\sigma$ limits. As long as this condition obtains, the process is considered stable.

Why should managers care about any of this? For two reasons. First, because the size of the $\pm 3\sigma$ limits of a random process, or the size of the stable neighborhood of the state of a deterministic system is designed into the system. If it exceeds what the customer will accept, only management can change it. Second,

FIGURE 5–3

An Example of a Shewart Control Chart of Product Sampled Daily

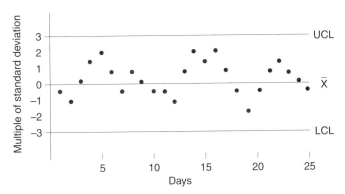

Shewart charts are now no longer limited to manufacturing processes, but have been demonstrated as applicable to services, military, financial, and social systems. What this means is inescapable—all processes behave this way; a manager cannot ignore his responsibility to stable operation.

Notice also that we refer to an equilibrium state as being either stable or not stable. No mention is made of whether the system itself is stable or unstable. This is because only linear systems have an inherent stability or not; nonlinear systems have stable or unstable equilibrium states. As managers, we don't care about whether our industrial process is linear or not, but our concern is simply whether it has a stable operational state.

MODELING

The Book of Genesis tells us that in the beginning, God created the universe from nothing. We marvel at His works, all the more because we have never been able to create something from nothing, not even the smallest speck. According to Plato, even our ideas are created from sensual perceptions of that which already exists.[2] Necessarily, then, when we want to create or design something, we model. We imagine in our mind's eye some design that is a translation of some other image, and develop it to suit our desire. This is not to say that brainstorming is a waste of time, or that all improvement must be incremental. New ideas and designs can be radical, completely innovative. But they derive from existing images. We want to design robust processes. This means that they adjust to disturbances or to innovations in order to maintain or achieve a product with desirable quality attributes. The processes adjust to change. Therefore, the mathematical models must have the property of convergence. There are many such models available, and in the following paragraphs we shall discuss several of them in general terms, in order to show how convergence is arrived at.

Generally, system models are mathematical, not physical. The reason for this is that systems are often too large to physically build at the beginning of design. This would be costly if we had to iterate many times, which is the usual case. In many cases it would be impossible to build a prototype, particularly if the process to be modeled were a social one or a large business enterprise. So we have the idea of the process in our mind's eye, it is abstracted to its mathematical essentials, then we can use analytical methods to pursue the design. A mathematical model provides the design precision in definition. Given the nature of this book, we will try not to get bogged down in mathematical detail, for two reasons. First, the purpose of the discussion is to present general concepts of models that may be appropriate to some design, at present unspecified. Second, mathematics carries its own rigorous language; understanding of that language is not a prerequisite for this book.

As you might suppose, just as there are deterministic and stochastic processes, there are also deterministic and stochastic models. We use models to effect the design of a desired process. Continuous time and discrete time models are described by differential equations and difference equations, respectively. With the exception of some simple queue models, the state trajectories of discrete event models are usually nonanalytic and often have no closed-form solution. Simulation is often used to find solutions with discrete event models.

We do not always associate the models one-on-one with the process that we want to model. For example, we may want to model a continuous time process such as the gypsy moth migration, but intend to take samples only periodically as a matter of convenience. In this case, we shall construct a discrete time model using difference equations. Modern modeling techniques now assure that difference and differential equations will provide the same results.

Discrete event processes can be modeled by deterministic models. Why would you want to? Because deterministic models have closed-form solutions. They are no better than the model, but then, neither is the solution of a simulation. For example, a manufacturing process is clearly a discrete process—output is generated in integer values, and a production level or inventory level might be considered a state of the system. Moreover, a change in state is due to an event, say final assembly or inspection. Disruptions are caused by events, say delayed parts delivery. Nevertheless, the process can be modeled as a function of time and the model can return useful results in terms of floor layout, inventory method, production process, and decision making. In order to use a time-driven model in place of an event-driven process, we assume that the process changes state primarily as a function of time, events occur on schedule, and events that can disturb it are small in impact.

Most discrete event modeling is used for processes subject to random events, but can be used for processes with scheduled events in which randomness occurs from time to time and has significant impact on the process. This kind of modeling is simply an attempt to deal with unpredictability in a systematic way. Most randomness follows a known distribution, and once it is identified, orderliness can be brought to the process. A simple example of this is found in queuing theory. We manage a branch bank in competition with other branches and other banks. If our customers are dissatisfied with the amount of time that they spend in line in our bank, they may go elsewhere. Conversely, we may win new customers if word gets out that our lines are fast. A queuing model will show us when and how many servers to provide to our customers.

We usually think of a project as a sequence of events that are driven by time. Many scheduling models exist to establish the optimum sequence and the critical path. But it often happens that the critical path is a period of time driven by events. Some industries, such as ship repair, suffer so greatly from resource perturbations that preproject scheduling is sometimes meaningless. Using a discrete event model for projects that are subject to event disturbances would enable us to put bounds on the schedule. We would determine the critical path of the project through conventional means, but then treat work item duration as random variables with mean *and* variance. (The variance must be included in the model. A work item with short mean duration and wide variance can be a schedule killer.) Then the sensitivity of the path to these statistics can be analyzed through computer simulation. By iteration, we arrive at the optimum critical path based upon the most probable schedule of work items.

ZEROING IN ON THE TARGET

There is no more appropriate expression for robustness than the old infantry phrase "zero in on the target." It may not be elegant, but it is exactly what we want to do. As Arora (1989) puts it, "the design of systems can be *formulated as problems of optimization,* where a measure of performance is to be optimized while satisfying all the constraints" (italics his). The robust design process is invariant to the kind of system desired, deterministic or random, and to the method of optimization used. The robust process is shown succinctly and clearly in Figure 5–4. The design variables in this figure are either the state variables (quality attributes) themselves, or they are variables that can indirectly enhance the quality attributes. They should be chosen to be mutually independent as far as possible.[3]

An objective function is an expression of some kind that contains the design variables, relating them to a goal, and is the most difficult part of the design process to formulate. The objective function must be considered with care because it is this function that will be optimized, and it is this function that will make it possible to delineate the best of several designs. It is often a mathematical, linear combination of design variables, but it doesn't have to be either linear or mathematical. At least it doesn't have to start out that way. At some point, though, it must result in either a scalar or utility value so that one design can be evaluated as better or worse than another. When the CEO says, "I want to cut customer complaints in half by next fiscal year," that is the makings of an objective function.

When the objective function is composed, each variable can be assigned a weight, a scale factor, or both. The scale factor comes

F I G U R E   5–4

Convergence through an Optimum Design Process

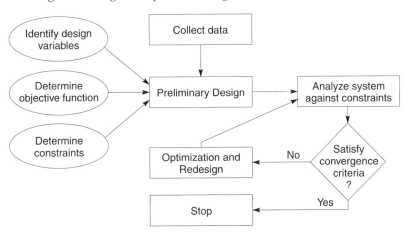

first and assures equal influence of all the design variables, irrespective of their range. For example, assume that we have an
objective function for the improvement of a distribution service,
and that it contains two design variables to be minimized. One
represents the average time of delivery, with an expected value of
two days, whereas the other represents the volume of pieces lost
weekly, with an expected value of 10,000 pieces. Clearly, the dis-
parity in their range of values is not indicative of their importance.
On the other hand, once we have scaled the variables to achieve
technical balance, it might be that we regard them as varying in
importance, subjectively. For example, we might consider that
reducing the number of lost pieces is the best way to increase customer volume. Weighting each variable provides a way of establishing greater or lesser influence to it.

The constraints of Figure 5–4 are expressions that contain the
design variables, but limit them in some way. There are always
constraints—for example, cost—but they must be put into the
design configuration. These constraints affect the state space of
the design by excluding regions that cause the variables to exceed
constraint limits. All of the state space that lies within the constraint boundaries is called the feasible region. The feasible region
will often contain satisfactory design solutions; the purpose of

an optimization process is to pick the best solution (set of values of the design variables). There will be satisfactory solutions outside the feasible region also, perhaps the best. But since the constraints are violated, such options are excluded. As an example, suppose that we want to optimize sales of a new automobile, but do not want to compete with a similar, smaller model that we ourselves manufacture. In this case, we would formulate an expression combining the design variables subject to the constraint that the result must exceed a given automobile weight. There may be profitable designs with less weight, but they would compete with our own small model, and so are not in the feasible region.

The data we collect serve three purposes. First, we want to establish whether the design variables are random or deterministic. Second, we want to bound their range. Third, we want to get some indication of their regions of independence. In our example service company, there must be some empirical upper and lower limits to the delivery time from which we can establish a reasonable range and tentative target value. Moreover, for substantially lower values of delivery time, we might find higher values of lost pieces, which is another of our design variables. There would be, in this case, dependence between the two variables, a condition that we do not want.

Following the preliminary design, we analyze the results to see if there has been an improvement within the feasible region. The objective function is reevaluated with the new values of the design variables, using an optimization technique; then redesign is accomplished. This process continues as long as improvement obtains, to the point of diminishing returns, or to the point of a predetermined target value. We thus arrive at the optimum system state, if there is one. Then we need to determine if this state is stable. This is easy to do using state space models because state space is literally a topology of system behavior, analogous to the topology of a three-dimensional geography. So, using analytical techniques, we examine the topology of the neighborhood in which the optimum point lies to determine whether the state (point in state space) is stable or not. If it is not, then we must abandon this state and look for another equilibrium.

There are a wide variety of optimization methodologies, and their selection depends upon the problem at hand. Are the design

T A B L E   5–1

Some Optimization Methodologies

Type of Design Variable	Optimization Method
Deterministic	Linear programming
	Dynamic programming
	Nonlinear programming
Random	Regression
	Markov decision process
	Response surface
	Design of experiments
Any type	Simulation

variables deterministic or random? Is the process linear or nonlinear? What is the form of the system in terms of objectives, resources, and constraints? Can the problem be posed in closed form, or is simulation required? A list of the genre is shown in Table 5–1. Within each category there are innumerable techniques. For example, nonlinear programming includes all those models for which linear programming and dynamic programming either do not apply or are inefficient. Design of experiments (DOE) is a general term for many different search strategies, among them analysis of variance (ANOVA) and factorial design. The following paragraphs are devoted to a brief discussion of the characteristics of each methodology. Sorting the infinitude of optimization techniques by genre is a rather arbitrary process. My rationale for this list is discussed in the Notes.[4]

Linear Programming.   The most common application of linear programming (LP) involves the general problem of allocating limited resources among competing activities in an optimal way. Suppose that we manufacture a half-dozen different products, all produced in the same factory, but made from different raw materials and purchased parts. Perhaps we make furniture: dining tables, chairs, bookcases, coffee tables, and end tables. Raw materials are maple, walnut, oak, and pine. Each product has a different demand and each raw material a different cost. Linear programming can identify the optimum production volume for each item.

LP does not refer to computer programming, but to a systematic planning iteration. An optimum design process involving linear objective and constraint functions is a candidate for this methodology. As with all the categories of Table 5–1, LP is both an optimization technique and a genre. Some of the better-known techniques contained within this category are simplex method, integer programming, goal programming, and network planning. Hillier and Lieberman (1990) believe that it is one of the most important scientific advances of the 20th century. Fundamental to operations research, various LP methods have saved millions of dollars in industrial applications over the past quarter century.

Dynamic Programming. As with LP, dynamic programming (DP) is concerned with the efficient allocation of resources, and is used in multidecision processes. Its power lies in its ability to converge to an optimal sequence of interrelated decisions. DP is a form of network planning in which an optimal policy is associated with each state or node. Suppose that we build custom automobiles, and that there is seasonal variation. Skilled labor, raw materials, and purchased parts are our resources. Seasonal fluctuation, overtime in peak periods, and layoff in slow periods are problems requiring decisions based upon conditions of the moment. Our basic policy is to resist mass layoffs as a poor strategy even in downsized markets because of the difficulty of finding skilled labor. This policy is offset by another against arbitrary overtime in peak seasons. Dynamic programming can minimize costs (or maximize profits) by determining the best decision to make at a given juncture of market, time, resources, and policy.

Although, as in LP, there are specific techniques called dynamic programming, I classify DP as a genre because any optimization technique that we use can be considered dynamic programming if the model requires that an optimal decision be made at each node of the network. Problems that are candidates for dynamic programming are those for which the *principle of optimality* applies: given the current state, the optimal policy for the remaining stages is independent of the policy adopted in previous stages. This is analogous to the Markov property, in that we can make the best decision based on present information.[5]

Nonlinear Programming. This is a catch-all genre of methods other than linear programming and its derivatives, that rely upon gradient searching techniques in a design space created by variables that are nonlinearly related. A simple but pertinent example is the quality loss function discussed in Chapter 1, in which cost of quality is nonlinearly related to deviation from target value. We should want a model capable of compensating for deviation in proportion to the displacement or rate of displacement from nominal, the compensation being in terms of time, resources, and perhaps policies.

Regression.[6] A regression equation is a mathematical expression used to represent the pattern of random data. The method optimizes this equation relative to random data by minimizing the errors due to regression and the errors due to randomness. Since regression is also used in measurement, a more detailed discussion is held in Chapter 7.

Markov Decision Processes. Suppose that we have an industrial or business process that can be described as a system with states and that it has two particular characteristics: (1) it is a random process with probabilities of being in any particular state, and (2) its probability of transiting to another state does not depend upon previous events. This is a Markov process. Many large projects fit this model for several reasons. The first is that the longer a project exists, the more likely that randomness will occur in the progress. Events such as inclement weather, logistics complexity, coordination of agents and activities, or labor strife all tend to a degree of randomness over extended time. The second reason that large projects tend to a Markovian nature is that the longer the time between two events, the less influence they have on each other. Thus, work item "A" may be required in order to go on to work item "B," but by the time we get to work item "N," the less "A" matters, and the more likely it is that going on to work item "P" depends only upon being on work item "N." This reality is de facto Markovian. Markov behavior is well understood and decision-making techniques have been developed for these processes based upon the state of the system at any given time.

Response Surface. .We have noted several times in this chapter that a set of state variables can be used to describe a space. Figure 5–2 demonstrates a three-dimensional space in which, by assuming any combination of values of the three attributes, we can arrive at any desired "point" in this space. That point will be a system state if the attributes are state variables. The attributes of Figure 5–2 could just as easily be factors, and the point a random variable whose value depends upon the values of the factors. A random variable that is dependent upon one or more factors is called a *response variable,* and the surface generated by all possible values of the factors is called a *response surface.* The response surface technique is a statistical analogy to the optimization techniques of deterministic systems. Assume that a manufacturer of clear plastic film is concerned with opaque spots appearing on his product during the production process. Factors of production are determined to be dryer temperature, process line speed, and film tension. He might then use a response surface method for determining the best settings of those factors to minimize the occurrence of the spots.

An important strategy of this technique is that the values are varied several at a time rather than the traditional one-at-a-time process. Box, Hunter, and Hunter (1978), for example, have shown that with some surfaces, a one-variable-at-a-time search will miss the optimum. Our manufacturer can take advantage of this relatively new idea and greatly reduce the number of experiments that must be run in order to determine optimum settings.

Design of Experiments.   DOE is a true genre and not a technique at all. There is no optimization technique called design of experiments. Rather, DOE refers to any statistical design procedure used to identify the factors that cause variation in quality of production or service. Two well-known techniques in this category are Analysis of Variance and Factorial Design.

Simulation.[7]   When a system is too complex to model analytically, a computer simulation may be a possible alternative. Simulation is done on a wide variety of processes: manufacturing, aerodynamic, weaponry, socioeconomic, and so on. There are several kinds of simulation, and they correspond closely to our categories of processes. A discrete event, or *Monte Carlo* simulation, is a model of

F I G U R E   5–5

Ship Repair Critical Path Simulation

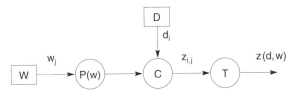

Legend:
  W = The specification
  w = A work item of the specification
  P(w) = Probability distribution of on time completion
  D = Decision set
  C = Transformation: D x W → Z
  Z = Outcome set
  T = Transformation: Z → Schedule

a process in which time plays no role—it is entirely event driven. There are also deterministic and stochastic simulation models. An example from Stimson (1993) is shown in Figure 5–5, in which a shipyard is to repair a vessel. The work to be done is described in a package of work items called the Specification. Each work item of the package is indicated by w_j.

Each work item on the critical path requires a certain period for completion, and the simulation assigns a probability based on the assumption that a 40-hour-week progression can be kept up about 65 percent of the time. The decision process allows management to apply resources as needed, or not, to maintain the critical path. Positive management action is required to ensure that materials arrive when needed, overtime or extra manpower is scheduled, critical resources and skills are on hand, and cash or credit is available to pay for them.

Figure 5–6 shows the result of this simulated activity. In the figure, the state of the repair, a random variable, is in terms of negative float on the critical path. Because of indecision, some work items are incomplete and negative float increases nonlinearly. The increase is slow at first, misleading management as to the impact of poor decision support. By the time that the schedule is clearly in trouble, it takes herculean efforts to save it.

F I G U R E   5–6

Simulation Results: Geometric Increase in Negative Float Due to Indecision

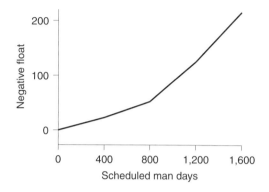

As for the simulation itself, the result is an average of thousands of computer iterations of the scenario, a large number of runs being needed in order to get meaningful statistical results from the probability distribution. There is a subtlety in this simulation, which appears to be indexed to time, and would therefore be a stochastic process. After all, the x-axis is in terms of man days. In fact, this is a Monte Carlo simulation because the scenario is event driven, the events being work item completions. The axes are, actually, accumulated negative float versus accumulated man days, both as a function of work item completions.

Figure 5–7 represents another simulation, that of an assembly line layout. Although seemingly simple, the model is complex because all process and transit times are random variables, each with its own distribution. The order of the jobs must follow the most efficient order of assembly, but distances, paths, transport type, and priorities are all strategies that can be optimized through computer iterations of the problem. This typical industrial application shows the power of simulation in optimization of complex problems.

Simulation, of course, can be applied to high-level managerial problems, also. For example, Luenberger (1979) discusses an analytic model of Richardson's theory of arms races, using an iterative, but closed-form model with difference equations. The model uses constants to represent intensities of reaction, fatigue, and

FIGURE 5–7

Simulated Floor Layout of a Manufacturing Assembly Line, Including
Transit Times, Random Delays, Process Times, Queues, and Interferences

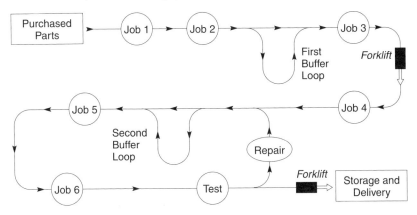

expanding costs. A realistic model would use random variables
rather than constants; therefore, the armament levels would have
probabilistic as well as deterministic components. The resulting
model could best be solved through computer simulation, perhaps using one of the many off-the-shelf simulation programs
already available. Even video simulations are now on the market.
Two excellent books on building complex simulations are listed
in the references: Pegden et al. (1990) and Law and Kelton (1991).

Simulation has its naysayers. Some critics say that simulation
is too complicated, with each added parameter introducing more
error. But the more complex the process, the more necessary modeling becomes, and analytical models are often too unresponsive.
Other critics say that simulation is too simple; the real world is
much more complex. But as Forrester (1969) pointed out, many of
these critics will spend billions based on their conclusions from a
simple one-input–one-output model that they keep in their heads.
Simulation was wildly successful in the early NASA days under
the Germans. Von Braun's team absolutely insisted on simulations
of all their aerospace flights. The model was complicated—a 23rd
order differential equation. But the success rate was 100 percent
through the Mercury, Gemini, and Apollo programs.

Up to now, the discussion on process dynamics has been general and nontechnical. Obviously, the key to convergence lies in an optimization method, but understanding and selecting a method requires a certain technical know-how. Is this detail really within the scope of management? Perhaps not the execution, but certainly the understanding. Box and Bisgaard (1988) point out that American management's understanding of statistical design has been limited, while Japanese managers require that these methods be used to develop high-quality processes. Bhote (1991) notes *endemic* variation in industrial processes, and lists its sources, causes, and means to reduction. He says that one way is top management training in overview of DOE.

Is Bhote correct in his assessment, or does he exaggerate? The argument about how much management should know of the nuts and bolts of a business is an old one, and will not be settled here. Hays and Wheelwright (1984) discuss the increasing use of professional managers in industry, without any special expertise in a company's markets or technology, who step into an unfamiliar company or division with the task of running it effectively. More often than not, these managers come from financial or legal backgrounds, and not from marketing, production, or engineering. The authors point out that not only is this trend contrary to European and Japanese practices, but accenting financial and legal skills, has led to the redefinition of the corporation as an entity for acquisition rather than production. I believe that the appropriate position of management in the nitty-gritty of production is as suggested by Bhote—they shouldn't do it but they should understand the process. In the next section, we will present an overview of one DOE technique—factorial design at two levels.

IMPLEMENTATION

The first step in improvement of process is to identify the process. What does it do, and how does it do it? In particular, how is change manifested? Does the process change continualiy? Can we see the changes continually, or only discretely? In what kind of environment does the process operate? Are there random influences? In answering these questions, we can begin to understand the dynamics involved, and consider, intelligently, how to get the process to do what we want, which is to converge to a target value. The second step is to recognize what it is we want to change. In short, we must identify the state and define our state variables. The rule of thumb is to select as many as are needed and no more.

We are interested in quality improvement, but the system state variables are not necessarily quality attributes. For example, the quality attribute of a machined piston might be the exactness of its diameter, time after time. Suppose that this exactness is directly related to the speed of the lathe. We might, then, designate lathe speed as our state variable. In this case, the quality attribute becomes an output variable of the system, directly related to system state. As another example of the intricacies of input-state-output identity, suppose that we have a bakery specializing in pies. It's pretty clear that there are multiple inputs—the pie ingredients. The pie is baked, then sold. But what is the state variable? The output can be considered either the fineness of the pie or the pleasure of the customer. There are probably two state variables, the heat of the oven and the time of baking. This simple example shows that you need to think about what will best serve as state variables—a quality characteristic or a process dynamic.

The repair of a fighting ship of the United States Navy is a good example of a large process in which a state is to be determined. The repair work to be done is usually in the form of a project, shown in Figure 5–8, involving hundreds of work items and hundreds of thousands of man hours of skilled labor. The complexity of the job has been observed by Pettavino (1989) in this way: "No other construction or manufacturing process even approximates the building and repair of large complex vessels." In such a complex evolution, there may be several ways to describe the state of the process; those shown in the figure represent one possible set of state variables.

In Figure 5–8, the specification is the set of work items that compose the repair. There are only four state variables: negative float, delayed materials, incomplete tests, and failed inspections. Although they all have different units, they can be expressed in the common unit of man days lost, and they are posed so that the objective of the multiple criteria decision system (management) is

F I G U R E   5–8

A Model of a Ship Repair Process with State Variables

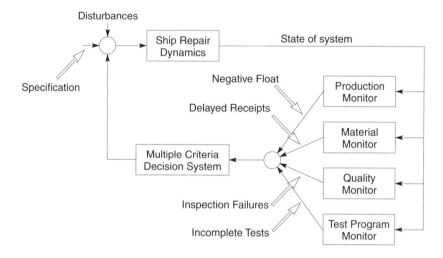

to minimize them. These variables are not unique; others might be selected. It is my view, however, that when these measurements are minimal, the quality of the product is maximized, and no other measurement need be made.

Having decided upon the nature of the process and how to describe its state, the next step is to determine an appropriate model. We ask many of the same questions that we posed in determining the nature of the process, the difference being two: (1) the model will be a simplification, and (2) it must be measurable. We can measure either the state variables or the system outputs if there is a one-to-one relationship between them. If it is cost effective to sample the process rather than to take continuous measurements, the model will be in discrete time. Policies must be established concerning sample frequency, size, and period. A rule of thumb is that the sampling frequency should be at least 10 times the frequency of the changing process. If the model is stochastic, then the rules of statistical evidence pertain. The next move is to select an appropriate optimization method. Factorial design is one of the methods under the DOE category, and is discussed in the next paragraph for demonstration.

Factorial Design

Even a single-state variable, if continuous, would have an infinite number of values. Infinity cannot be measured. The need to have at least *some* quantitative information about a process is inescapable. Getting this information is what data collection of Figure 5–4 is all about. We must bound the enterprise. One way in which we can do this is through an experimental design method called *Factorial Design*. Before discussing this method, let's clarify some names.

We have already defined state variables as those parameters that tell us, quantitatively, what a system or process is doing. Design variables are those parameters that we can observe and measure in order to determine their best values for an effective design. It is very convenient when the state and design variables are the same thing, but that is not always the case. Finally, another term comes into play: *factors*. This name comes from the statistical world, which often has its own vocabulary. For our purposes a factor is an independent variable and can be likened to a state variable.

Assume that we have established the range of interest of the state variables or factors in the experiment. There is still an immensity of space to explore. For example, if there were only three factors and we wanted to run tests at ten settings of each factor, then we would need to run 1,000 tests, a very large number for so few factors. Let's choose an even simpler case for purposes of demonstration. Assume that we still have just three factors: dryer temperature, line speed, and film tension. We want to run tests at only two settings of each factor. Then eight tests are needed. If the settings are selected wisely, the state space is bounded as shown in Figure 5–9. In the figure, Q1 through Q8 are the values of the response variable, say the number of spots per square yard of clear film, taken at each triplet of settings. For example, Q1 is the number of spots measured when all three factors are at their lowest setting. Q4 is the number of spots measured when temperature and film tension are at their highest setting, and line speed at its minimum. This strategy of varying the levels of the factors is the more efficient because they are varied simultaneously rather than one at a time, but the variation is systematic. The set of values are tabularized with the various levels of each factor, then the table is

---

F I G U R E   5–9

A Boxed Volume of State Space of Three Variables

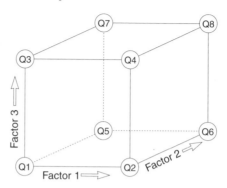

analyzed to detect trends and interactions. Since the number of spots per square yard is a random variable, it will be necessary to run iterations of each test to arrive at an average value of the number of spots for each triplet of settings.

The advantages of factorial design are, first, that the number of experiments or tests is reduced, and second, that the attribute we wish to optimize is determined by simultaneous settings of all the factors that contribute to it. Historically, optimization was done one variable at a time. Box, Hunter, and Hunter (1978) have shown that when interrelationships exist among the factors, the optimum value of the desired attribute can be missed. The disadvantage of the technique is that a great deal must be known about the state space.

Chapters 4 and 5 provide techniques that enable a robust process design that will maintain the target value of a designated quality characteristic irrespective of perturbations. The same mechanism that provides convergence of the process to a target value also provides convergence to *any* desired value within the capability of the system, so that improvement is possible simply by selecting a new objective. We begin robust design by determining what our goal is, and figure out the best way to approach the design process itself. Once that chore is finished, we are ready to examine process dynamics and the important question of stability. We define a state of the process. This must be done *before* a model is selected.

We want the state of the process, not the state of the model. Having established state variables, we are then ready to incorporate a convergence mechanism into the model and begin the optimization program. This completes the design of the process and leads to the next step, and the next chapter, on how to control it.

N O T E S

1. **Dynamic Process.** I want to avoid both redundancy and misunderstanding. The term *dynamic process* seems redundant because our intuitive understanding of a process is that it is a dynamic mechanism. At the same time, we employ Kalman's definition of a system as a dynamic concept. But we have adopted the convention, in this book, that a process and a system are the same thing. Thus, we have *dynamic* associated with *process* intuitively, and associated with *system* by definition. Further complication comes in because some savants, such as Luenberger (1979), insist that a dynamic system is one that is time-evolutionary, and some, such as Ho and Cao (1991), insist that discrete event systems are dynamic also. The solution is to adopt a consistent policy within the book. Our convention: any process that is capable of changing state is dynamic.

2. **Creativity.** In his *Dialogues,* Plato explores the elements of creativity, dividing them into two parts, divine and human. He denies that nature has been created by a spontaneous and unintelligent cause, but rather, is the work of God. The human part of creativity is again divided into two parts, the imaginative and the productive. The notion that a creative work has two manifestations, one in our mind and one physical, although fascinating, is not germane here. We are concerned with Plato's idea that humans create from imagination, which is stimulated by the senses. Therefore, human creation is a translation of what exists to another thing that exists.

3. **Optimization and State Space.** The idea of treating independent variables as coordinate axes in space comes from the work of physicists in studying the kinetic energy of gases. The space was called the phase plane. In the 1950s engineers, requiring an efficient means of analyzing complex systems with multiple inputs and outputs, adapted the method to hyperspace, that is, the n-dimensional space created by independent variables that represented the state of the system under study. This hyperspace was called, naturally enough, the system state space. Optimization refers to the analytical techniques used to find peaks and valleys in state space—that is, maxima and minima. A

simple example of the utility of this practice can be imagined by considering the time-fuel problem of sounding rockets. You want to maximize the amount of their time in space and minimize the amount of fuel that they consume.

4. **Optimization Techniques.** Sorting the many methods by genre is a rather arbitrary process. For example, dynamic programming is a form of network planning; therefore, it belongs to the genre of networking, as does the well-known critical path management (CPM). But linear programming is also a type of network planning, yet it is so important that it must be recognized explicitly in any serious claim to sorting. I would rather list CPM and other kinds of networking under the genre of dynamic planning, and designate LP as its own genre.

5. **Principle of Optimality and the Markovian Property.** A Markovian system is a stochastic process in which state transition has no memory, that is, the probability of moving from one state to another does not depend on previous events. This behavior is called the *Markovian property*. The *Principle of Optimality* is expressed in different forms, but one that is easily understood is that of Hillier and Lieberman (1990): knowledge of the current state of the system conveys all the information about its previous behavior necessary for determining the optimal policy henceforth. Thus, a system that lacks the Markovian property cannot be formulated as a dynamic programming problem.

6. **Regression.** This is another term that has, apparently, a different meaning to statisticians than it has among the general population. This time, however, we know its origin. The name comes from Sir Francis Galton (1822–1911), an experimenter and statistician, who used it in the general sense, observing that children's heights regressed toward the average height of the population rather than digressing from it. The statistical model that he used came to be known as regression analysis, or simply regression. Box, Hunter, and Hunter (1978) call it the method of least squares, this being the usual method to fit the equation to the data.

7. **Simulation.** The author worked for IBM in Huntsville, Alabama, during the period of space vehicle development, while Wernher Von Braun was director of NASA's Marshall Space Flight Center. In addition to Von Braun, most of the Center's top management were all German. Although IBM succeeded in getting this management to accept some digital computer simulations, the Germans insisted on analog computer simulations to provide the basis of evidence. The reasons are too technical to interest the general reader.

REFERENCES

AMA Forum. "How American Express Measures Quality of Its Customer Service." *AMA Forum Management Review,* American Management Association, March 1982, pp. 29–31.

Arora, Jasbir. S. *Introduction to Optimum Design.* New York: McGraw-Hill, 1989.

Bhote, Keki R. *World Class Quality.* New York: AMACOM, a division of the American Management Association, 1991.

Box, G. E. P., and Soren Bisgaard. "Statistical Tools for Improving Designs." *Mechanical Engineering,* January 1988, pp. 32–40.

Box, G. E. P.; William G. Hunter; and J. Stuart Hunter. *Statistics for Experimenters.* New York: John Wiley & Sons, 1978.

Forrester, Jay W. *Urban Dynamics.* Cambridge, MA: MIT Press, 1969.

Hayes, Robert H., and Steven C. Wheelwright. *Restoring Our Competitive Edge: Competing through Manufacturing.* New York: Copyright © 1984 John Wiley. Reprinted by permission of John Wiley & Sons, Inc.

Hillier, Frederick S., and Gerald J. Lieberman. *Introduction to Operations Research.* New York: McGraw-Hill, 1990.

Ho, Yu Chi, and Xi Ren Cao. *Perturbation Analysis of Discrete Event Dynamic Systems.* Boston: Kluwer Academic Publishers, 1991.

Law, Averill M., and W. David Kelton. *Simulation, Modeling, and Analysis.* New York: McGraw-Hill, 1991.

Lovelock, Christopher H. "Federal Express Quality Improvement Program." Case study of the Sloan School of Management, Massachusetts Institute of Technology. Copyright 1990 by the International Institute for Management Development, Lausanne, Switzerland.

Luenberger, David G. *Introduction to Dynamic Systems.* New York: John Wiley & Sons, 1979.

Pegden, C. Dennis; Robert E. Shannon; and Randall P. Sadowski. *Introduction to Simulation Using SIMAN.* New York: McGraw-Hill, 1990.

Pettavino, Paula J. "Prospects for Shipyard Mobilization: The Shipbuilding Industry and the U.S. Navy in Peace and War." *Naval Engineers Journal,* January 1989, pp. 45–65.

Plato. *The Sophist.* The Great Books. Chicago: Encyclopaedia Britannica, 1952.

Šiljak, Dragoslav D. *Nonlinear Systems.* New York: John Wiley & Sons, 1969.

Stimson, William A. "Statistical Quality Control and Navy Ship Repair." *Naval Engineers Journal,* January 1993, pp. 59–65.

6

⑥   PROCESS ORGANIZATION

ORGANIZING THE ORGANIZATION

Organizational reengineering is based on two interacting factors: total customer satisfaction and effective and efficient internal processes. A company's success depends upon its ability to satisfy customers' needs. In turn, this ability depends on how well the organization's internal processes work to meet this external demand. Therefore, the organization succeeds from the inside out.

J. N. Lowenthal, 1994

Lowenthal's comments are exactly in tune with the thrust of this chapter—organizing processes. First, however, we have to rid ourselves of an ambiguity. The quote uses the term *organization* as a proper noun. This practice is fairly common in the United States at least, and as the heading of this paragraph suggests, we see three common usages:

"Let's organize these processes effectively."
"Our processes are arranged into an effective organization."
"Our organization is one of the Fortune 500."

The last usage treats *organization* as a particular one, and therefore a proper noun. It carries with it a weight and rigidity associated with institutions, and tends to impose a sense of permanence to the meaning of the word. This usage preempts the sense of flexibility and adaptability that is inherent in the verb *organize.* Thus the ambiguity. To get away from this, we will use the word *organization* only as a common noun as in the middle example, or as used in the title of this paragraph, or as used in the act of organizing, for example, *the organization of a company*. In this book, a particular organization is called a company.

In earlier chapters, we discussed how to design stable, controllable processes in terms of general structure. With the exception of design control, we discussed no particular kinds of processes, only the form that a robust process should have. In this chapter we will discuss ways to organize particular processes into an effective whole: how to organize the *company*. We will begin by reviewing critiques on certain entrenched structures offered by recognized experts in the field, then proceed to advance some ideas of our own. We will demonstrate the implementation of these ideas with example organizations for commonly performed functions.

OSSIFYING THE ORGANIZATION

If you're going to organize processes, what do you organize them around? What is the basis? The most common structure is around function, and this is often displayed as an organization chart. This sort of arrangement is called a line organization, and is a favorite target of critics, so it is worthwhile to review what they have to say. Pascarella and Frohman (1989) state that with the passage of time, stagnation sets in as management spends too much time on old technology and develops more layers of hierarchy. This occurs because innovation comes from people with entrepreneurial personalities that clash with function. Function tends to focus on activities rather than results. Each function becomes an entity unto itself, creating a *rice bowl* concept. The problem with rice bowls is that if a task is regarded by a functional manager as "not in our charter," then it cannot get done because no one else in the company is authorized to do it. Several years ago, it was my job to conduct ship qualification trials of surface combatants of the United States Navy. The agency that I worked for was functionally organized about various weapons systems. We were authorized to train the crews in maintenance of their systems, but not in their operation. That was another rice bowl, and not always funded. However, the trials always culminated with live firings of the systems, crew trained or not. As a result, we trained the officers and crew in systems operations, and simply told no one about it.

When line organizations become ossified, Pascarella and Frohman note that people who want to get things done are then forced to operate outside the organizational boundaries. As an example, one of the last phases of system acquisition by the United States Navy is called technical evaluation. "TechEval" is considered an *imprimatur*,[1] that often gains with time, unfortunately, the status of *nihil obstat*. Following the sinking by Argentine forces of HMS *Sheffield*, in 1986, the U.S. Navy became concerned about defending its own ships against antiship missiles. I obtained resources to examine a cruiser's point defense capability. However, the functional organization with cruiser purview would not cooperate, on the grounds that its systems had already undergone TechEval (20 years earlier!). Without this vital cooperation of primary resources, we had to bootleg the sea trial and end up with inconclusive results.

Structures can be dysfunctional. Tomasko (1993) concludes that most organizational structures better represent their company's history than their promise. They are a result of old political adjustments and past strategies, and seldom provide a power base for critical capabilities. This circumstance comes about from benign and quite human forces. We eventually work our way up to our level of incompetence, tolerated because who wants to fire a man who has performed well over the years? On the other hand, criticality is found down where the rubber meets the road, in the market place—where the young, unconnected employee is dealing face to face with the customer. In order to resolve this kind of development, de facto lines of communication evolve that are not reflected on the organizational chart.

This view is reinforced by MacKenzie (1986), who demonstrates the existence in many organizations of the *virtual position*. In Chapter 4 we saw that, according to Mackenzie, the correspondence of line organizations as they appear on paper and as they operate is less than 50 percent, and that a good one would rate about 60 percent. A virtual position, then, is a position tasked to a process, but which has no immediate supervisor-subordinate chain. The task is getting done, but not according to the chart. This kind of organization gives rise to official and actual roles, and why should a customer pay for that?

The news on functional organization is not all bad, of course, just as Byzantine operations are not all bad. They're still with us, so they must have some saving grace. Rigby, quoted by Lowenthal (1994), lists some benefits of functional organization, among them: they maximize utilization of special skills; they offer cost-effective divisions of labor; and they offer economies of scale in plant and equipment. Organizations can be more effective in coordination and integration with *cross-functional* structure, such as matrix management. The problem with matrix management, according to Lowenthal, is that it often results in total confusion between managers as they attempt to shift from functional to cross-functional modes on an as-needed basis. In my own experience with matrix management, I've found that resources remain in control of the functional manager, so that the Golden Rule applies—he who has the gold, rules. The project manager often does not have the authority needed to get the job done. This is why the concepts of authority, responsibility, and accountability have been defined and highlighted in Chapter 4.

There are other ways to organize processes, too. In modern management control theory, processes are organized based on profit centers. Hays and Wheelwright (1984) note, however, that there is good and bad in profit center orientation. The good is obvious—quick response to market dynamics, both in terms of growth and in linear technology development. On the bad side, profit centers are less effective when faced with requirements for major process change, and also tend to encourage focus on the quarterly bottom line. So if we're not enthusiastic about organizing processes functionally or as profit centers, what's left? Well, the most change-sensitive organization is to organize around the processes themselves. Many authors endorse this idea, and we will review some of their comments, taking a similar tack, but with a robust twist.

DESIGNING THE ORGANIZATION

Ship repair yards are good examples of plants that can be process oriented but tend instead to functional organization. In principle, the work can flow naturally because the shops have process flow layouts and because the work is processed by job shop and group technology. The problem, however, is that although the work tends to flow, humanity tends to institutionalize. There are trades and shops and rules, all leading to the creation of barriers to flow and to definition of function. Good shipyards minimize functional constraints, but it takes extra effort. Chirillo (1990) presents one solution, and that is to redefine the work package by product line in such a way as to force an organized flow through the yard. The idea is to define the work by "product," that is, value-added activity, relative to the zone of a ship, as well as to the trades involved. This is a *force fit design*. It may achieve the process flow, but it does not address the fundamental problem of the plant's functional organization. It is analogous to the virtual position concept of getting things done by finding a way around the line organization.

Peter Keen's (1991) approach to organization begins with the issues of risk and complexity. In this sense, risk refers to the possibility that a technically functional innovation will fail to secure buy-in, threaten aspects of the firm's traditions and processes, or require skills that the organization does not have. Environmental complexity is that change in external forces that acts upon the company. It is often met with an increase in organizational complexity such as more management, procedures, reports, and controls, with an associated increase in overhead. Reliance on impersonal paper-based communication increases. The result is a host of pathologies. In most organizations, according to Keen, information technology has *added*, not reduced, complexity, as management information systems focus on the overhead activities. Information technology (IT) can reduce complexity significantly if used, not as a database, but to

1. Target organizational simplicity of work procedures and coordination.
2. Design structure- and location-independent organizations.
3. Facilitate the collaborative organization.
4. Repersonalize management.
5. Make it easier to communicate than not to do so.

Through the compatible use of IT, the *relational organization* is realized, which is defined not by fixed structure but by ease of relationships. But here again, easy relationships assume a process-oriented intellect behind the information technology, and do not address the fundamental problem of the plant's functional organization. The ideas of Chirillo and Keen are good, but will work even better if the organization is process structured.

One way of overcoming functional compartmentalization is to create flow charts, but Tomasko reports that this is a weak half-step unless the logic of the flow chart is transferred to the organization chart. He calls for abandoning the functional business unit and creating an organizational unit for each key process that produces a result for a customer. Hierarchies are maintained, but are determined by process times and not functional levels. Being dynamic, every process has a time constant or period of performance. Tomasko generates five levels of management according to time constants or periods.[2] Team leaders are concerned with processes of several months or less; business process managers with processes of about 1 year; enterprise unit managers with processes of 2 to 3 years; group executives with 5-year processes; and the top management team is concerned with processes of 10 years.

Supporting process organization, Ackoff et al. (1984) recommend structuring in terms of inputs, outputs, and management control systems. This should be done at all levels. At the top level, there are two distinct functions: one for strategy and one for operations. The company should be organized to facilitate efficient operations, to allow rapid response to changing conditions, and to clearly define accountability and responsibility. The organization should provide for policy setting at the top and decision making at the lowest possible level.

Ackoff's idea of control structures at all levels is put in a similar perspective by MacKenzie, who identifies two hierarchies: a hierarchy of task process levels and a hierarchy of aggregation. Task process levels are those of execution, supervising, and planning. MacKenzie's *level of aggregation*[3] refers to the detail of their description, and this is where the perspectives of Ackoff and MacKenzie approach our robust system. Refer again to Figure 1–3 of Chapter 1, showing a closed loop of connected functions. Each function is itself a closed-loop system. It is possible, even desirable, to have a number of nested closed loops. Every process should be closed, as should every subprocess. In another context, we quote DeMorgan's "A Budget of Paradoxes"[4]:

Great fleas have little fleas upon their backs to bite 'em,
And little fleas have lesser fleas, and so ad infinitum.

A robust system doesn't need an infinitude of closed loops, but every process must be closed. For example, in Figure 1–3 the process dynamics block has an improvement subsystem. The process dynamics block itself might be the entire company, a process within the company, or a subprocess, and so on. Imagine that you are viewing Figure 1–3 through a microscope with discrete power settings. At each level of magnification, you can focus on another level of aggregation. With robust systems, at each level you will see the structure of Figure 1–3.

MacKenzie measures the congruency and redundancy of an organization of processes. In determining congruency he tests for agreement between goals, strategies, task processes, environments, and results. In looking for redundancy of effort he tests for correspondence of the organization chart to the way the task processes have been assembled, to the communications network between activities, and to the allocation of resources among the activities. In a completely effective system, there would be no inadvertent redundancy. Each process would be serially dependent upon its predecessor process only.

The ideas that we've reviewed are good. They tell us what we should have, or having it, how to measure its effectiveness. But they don't tell us how to get there. That is no problem, though, because we know the answer already. We have an organization with the capabilities and that will satisfy the criteria we've been discussing. It is the organization shown in Figure 1–3, with one addition. Each of its subsystems should be organized as shown in Figure 6–1.

Let's see how the concerns of the preceding paragraphs are addressed by Figures 1–3 and 6–1. Organizational risk and environmental complexity are input at the *random disturbances* block of Figure 1–3, and detected and addressed by the improvement system. Organizational complexity is reduced by the simplicity of Figure 6–1, whose fundamental structure never varies, no matter what the process being implemented. We have created an organizational unit for each key process that produces a result for a customer. We have structured the organization in terms of inputs, outputs, and management control systems. Finally, with traceability, we can

F I G U R E   6–1

The Fundamental Process Model with Traceability

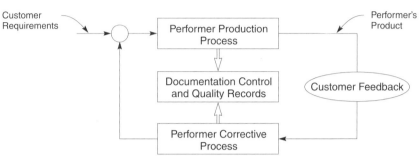

determine the congruency and redundancy of the organized processes. Figure 1–3 represents any arbitrary aggregate level. It can be blown up to discretely higher detail; variance from the ideal form of Figure 6–1 will be immediately obvious. Redundancy may not be obvious, but that is one of the reasons for documentation control and quality records.

As with all blocks in the figures, *documentation control and quality records* is a process also. Document vaults can be deadly places, as they represent stasis. The purposes of taking data at all are (1) to provide information about customer requirements and product improvement; (2) to provide statistics for analysis of process stability, capability, and improvement; and (3) to provide evidence of efficiency of operations and achievement of goals. More will be said about this critical issue later in this chapter because if not dynamic, documentation and records can be a progress arrestor, empire builder, and general all-around cement albatross. To borrow a term from physics, documentation and records can be a *sink*[5] if not used properly.

IMPLEMENTATION

Figure 6–1 represents a generalized form of how to organize a process. The best way to demonstrate how this general form is implemented is to give some examples. The following paragraphs discuss the implementation of processes found in almost any industry.

Contract Review

A common dictionary defines a contract as a formal agreement, usually written, between two parties. Thus, if one agrees to provide a product or service to a client, the contract between them defines its quality. To see this, recall how we derived our definition of quality in Chapter 1. "Conformance to specifications" was adapted from Crosby's "Conformance to requirements," the requirements being determined by the customer. It is extremely important, therefore, to get the requirements into the contract, clearly and totally. When the customer is involved in the formulation of the contract, then his expectations can be groomed according to the possible. This is where an agreement of expectations is established. But the contract formulation is only the beginning. Achieving quality requires a process of continual review of the contract until the product or service is delivered to the satisfaction of the customer. The purpose of contract review is to ensure that the requirements are adequately defined and documented, that differences between performer and customer are resolved, and that the company can do the job.

As Lamprecht (1993) notes, the nature of this review will vary according to the business. In a restaurant, for example, contract review is conducted between customer and waiter. A request of the customer for variance from the tender (menu) is agreed to. If the chef delivers a product that is nonconforming, then there is a procedure for resolving this also. If the business is that of software programs, then the process of contract review and of control of nonconforming product will involve a much longer time frame, and probably a more formal procedure. Irrespective of the business, the contract review process will take the closed-loop form shown in Figure 6–2. Notice that there are two feedback loops in the organization. One ensures an agreement of expectations before the performance begins. The other calls for a continual review of performance against contract requirements throughout the period of performance. This ensures a maturity of expectations. It often happens, especially in the achievement of complex work, that a particular objective or desire of the customer must be modified. It is always better that the customer be aware of this turn of events as soon as possible, together with the necessary trade-offs in alternative solutions or added costs in pursuing the difficulty.

F I G U R E   6–2

The Organization of a Contract Review Process

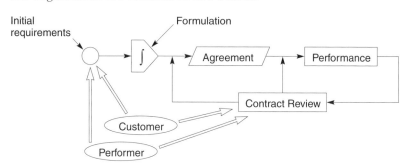

Customer satisfaction does not mean giving the customer what he wants. It means meeting or exceeding his expectations. Customer expectations are dynamic. If it becomes necessary to modify the performance or educate the customer, then his expectations must be modified also. This is what I mean by maturity of expectations. The contract review process organized as shown in Figure 6–2 accommodates dynamic expectations by involving the customer in the performance process. This is a *robust* organization as it converges to customer expectations.

Document Control and Quality Records

The way you systemize a process is through documentation. This provides repeatability. It also proves that you are doing what you say you're doing. In many industries, such as aerospace and pharmaceutical, document control is necessary because of the sheer volume of change orders or distribution of powerful chemicals. There are two particular concerns: appropriate documents must be available where needed, and inappropriate documents must be promptly removed from use. The latter is often difficult to achieve because of the propensity of people to retain familiar documents, for example, procedures, which may have personal notes on them, and because of the availability of copying machines. Nevertheless, a superseded document at a workstation can create nonconformities in the product and may therefore become a common cause.

Quality records should be considered an important subset of documentation and control. It is that documentation that maintains legible, identifiable, and retrievable records of performance characteristics relative to customer requirements. Quality records demonstrate achievement of the effective operation of the quality system. In keeping with our management responsibility of Chapter 3, quality records enable you to *"Say what you do; do what you say; prove it."*

In some companies, the quality operation of document control is elevated to functional status, often enjoying department-level prestige. This can make sense in some industries, but as a general rule I question whether it is a good idea. If possible, each function within the company should do its own document control, as indicated in Figure 6–1. There are three good reasons for this. First, raising document control to department level adds extraordinary status to what is essentially an overhead cost. Second, the functional group has functional expertise. They know what needs to be documented and what weight or credibility to give each document.

Third, the functional group is more likely to document all its work if it retains that work. It is less likely to turn over preliminary work documentation to a third party, say, a Department of Document Control. For example, in design, the early work deals with fuzzy requirements, parameters with undetermined metric, and brainstorming type ideas. Some of the ideas may prove to be simply poor and are rejected by the designers. Yet, it may turn out at some later stage that a previously rejected hypothesis might be promising if only one could remember why it was rejected. Documentation of earlier ideas provides corporate memory. Designers can be induced to retain this documentation *in-house,* but will hesitate to submit anything but final documents to nondesigners.

What happens, then, is that departments of documentation and control tend to be repositories for final and official documents. The people in-house seldom use it. So you wind up with two repositories—the pretty one and the *real* one. This is the antithesis of a quality process. Documentation and control should be viewed as an overhead *process* responsibility that can be organized within every functional process, as shown in Figure 6–1. This is a robust organization because it merges the two worlds: what you say you do and what you do.

Purchasing

Stahl and Grigsby (1992) note that, irrespective of slogans, the real mission of a company can be determined by its resource allocations. Thus, the requisition and distribution of resources may well define the company. Inventory is the state variable of purchasing. Inventory may be driven by a system of material requirements planning (MRP), economic order quantity (EOQ), just-in-time, or some other method appropriate to a business.

A quality purchasing process contains certain safeguards. It ensures that a purchased product conforms to specification, provides contractor assessment, and tracks purchasing status and data. It allows for customer verification of contractors and provides criteria for contractor selection. It maintains procedures for verification, storage, and maintenance of purchaser supplied product, which directly affects quality. Where appropriate, the quality purchasing process maintains procedures for identifying the product from applicable drawings, specifications, or other documents, during all stages of production, delivery, and installation. If traceability is required by the customer, then individual product or batches will have a unique, recorded identification. Often, traceability is a legal requirement as well as a quality factor, particularly in the case of pharmaceutical companies.

A closed-loop purchasing system such as that shown in Figure 6–3 contains the quality factors we've discussed and is robust because it converges inventory to dynamic demand, at the same time providing control of the quality factors.

Process Control

The heart of a manufacturing (or service) activity is the process used to make the product. Obviously, these processes should be the focus of management attention and tactical thinking. There are some fundamentals that apply to process control whether the product is manufactured or provision of service. To ensure that processes operate under controlled conditions, the company should provide written (or software-displayed) work instructions that are readable and current, and some means to monitor and control process and product characteristics should be provided.

A General Purchasing System with Inventory, Product, and
Contractor Controls

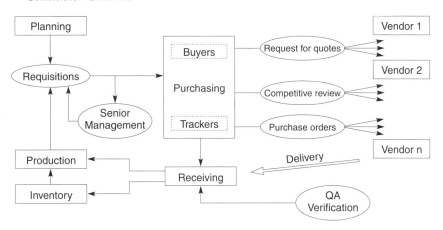

Availability of instructions makes worker substitution possible,
and a monitoring mechanism allows the worker to evaluate how
well he is doing. Modern quality theory promotes the idea that
each worker is responsible for his own quality. In-process quality
control is local. Of course the worker requires a standard or specification to which to perform, so that these references must be provided also. Usually, but not always, the job order contains the specifications that reflect customer requirements. If that is the case,
then the job order becomes the worker's standard. Following the
specifications of the job order connects work to quality and is the
reason why we adapted Crosby's definition of quality for our purposes. "Conformance to specifications" is down-to-earth and easily
understood on the factory floor.

     The workforce itself should be involved in the writing of
work procedures. The more experienced ones know how and why
they do something. A good idea is to generate flow diagrams of
the processes that will reveal the processes most likely to affect
quality. Some analysis will be required because most production
systems include many processes that are simply subprocesses of a
key process. Documenting the key process comprehensively will
be sufficient.

FIGURE 6–4

Process Control

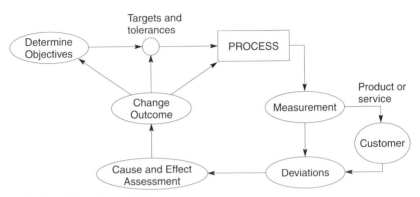

(Derived from Stahl and Grigsby, 1992)

Figure 6–4, adapted from Stahl & Grigsby (1992), indicates a closed-loop method of process control. Note that the customer is in the control loop, representing an input into deviations. The input may be a critical evaluation of the product, a desire for a change, or a request for a new concept. Note also that corrective actions reflect true flexibility—process parameters, target values, even objectives must be reviewed and changed, if necessary. Consistent with strategic thinking, only core values are fixed. Since the process is created to implement the values, all its parts must remain variables.

Through Chapter 6, we've developed methods to design and organize robust, stable processes, and have provided some examples. But we're operating in a blind environment (sometimes called a fool's paradise) without measuring what we're doing. In Chapter 7, we shall discuss the requirements and subtleties of measuring performance.

NOTES

1. *Imprimatur* **and** *Nihil Obstat.* Official documents of the Roman Catholic Church were released to the general public only after their content had been approved by the appropriate authority and received an *imprimatur.* Of course, the document had to be free of religious

error *nihil obstat.* I do not know if these steps are still required, but the statements have appeared on official Church documents for centuries and carry the weight of history. I use the terms here, not facetiously at all; on the contrary, to me they represent emphatic statements of final authority.

2. **Time Constant.** A process does something. Industrial processes usually do what they do repetitively. The period of time that it takes to perform one cycle of operation is one of the characteristics of the process. If the process is not periodic, then it is aperiodic. It can still be characterized by time, using a parameter that we may call its *time constant.* This term comes from electronics, and pertains to the period of time, which is fixed, that an exponential process takes to perform about 63 percent of its function. Whether an industrial process dynamic is exponential or not, it usually has a fixed element of time inherent in some aspect of its operation that is characteristic of it. It is useful to identify this parameter as its time constant. For example, suppose we have a punch press that is used for five different punching configurations, each configuration capable of processing sheets of steel at a fixed rate. Each job order varies in the size and configuration of the task, so that any sequence of job orders is effectively aperiodic. In this case the punch press has five time constants, each referring to a set-up time and process rate for a given configuration. This set of time constants is a characteristic of the press and a useful measure of its capability.

3. **Level of Aggregation.** MacKenzie defines levels of task processes in a hierarchy based upon intradependence. The lowest level is an *activity,* which contains no subprocesses. The next is a *module,* which is a set of activities with a common predecessor activity. A *bundle* is a set of modules with a common predecessor module; similarly, *group* and *area.* The structure does not ensure robustness, but does help to establish the reach of processes, and so is helpful to us in determining integration requirements.

4. **DeMorgan.** Augustus DeMorgan was a 19th century English logician of the first rank and contributor of an important theorem, used widely in logic, boolean algebra, and digital computer design.

5. **Sink.** In physics, a *sink* is a perfect absorber of energy, emitting none. A *source,* on the other hand, is a perfect emitter of energy, absorbing none. We have all had the great pleasure of knowing human sources; they cheer us up when we are weary. We remember them all our lives. We remember the sinks, too. We can usually survive sinks, but in a competitive environment, companies cannot.

REFERENCES

Ackoff, Russell L.; Jamshid Gharajedaghi; and Elsa Vergara Finnel. *A Guide to Controlling Your Corporation's Future.* New York: John Wiley & Sons, 1984.

Chirillo, Louis D., CDR. USN (Ret.). "Productivity: How to Organize the Management and Manage the Organization." *Naval Engineers Journal,* November 1990, pp. 26–34.

DeMorgan, Augustus. *A Budget of Paradoxes.* London: Longmans, Gree, & Co., 1872.

Hayes, Robert H., and Steven C. Wheelwright. *Restoring Our Competitive Edge: Competing through Manufacturing.* New York: Copyright © 1984 John Wiley. Reprinted by permission of John Wiley & Sons, Inc.

Keen, Peter G. W. *Shaping the Future.* Boston: Harvard Business School Press, 1991.

Lamprecht, James L. *Implementing the ISO 9000 Series.* New York: Marcel Dekker, Inc., 1993. Reprinted by courtesy of Marcel Dekker, Inc.

Lowenthal, Jeffrey N. *Reengineering the Organization: A Step-by-Step Approach to Corporate Revitalization.* Milwaukee, WI: ASQC Quality Press, 1994.

MacKenzie, Kenneth D. *Organizational Design: The Organization Audit and Analysis Technology.* Norwood, NJ: Ablex Publishing Corp., 1986.

Pascarella, Perry, and Mark A. Frohman. *The Purpose-Driven Organization.* San Francisco: Jossey-Bass Publishers, 1989.

Stahl, Michael J., and David W. Grigsby. *Strategic Management for Decision Making.* Boston: Copyright © 1992. PWS-Kent Publishing. Reproduced with the permission of Southwestern College Publishing, a division of International Thomson Publishing Inc. All rights reserved.

Tomasko, Robert M. *Rethinking the Corporation.* New York: Copyright © 1993. Reprinted with permission of the publisher, AMACOM, a division of the American Management Association.

7

⑥ THE MEASUREMENT PROCESS

THE COMPONENTS OF MEASUREMENT

I often say that when you can measure what you are speaking about and express it in numbers, you know something about it; but when you cannot measure it, when you cannot express it in numbers, your knowledge is of a meagre and unsatisfactory kind: it may be the beginning of knowledge, but you have scarcely, in your thoughts, advanced to the stage of science, whatever the matter may be.

William Thomson, Lord Kelvin, 1891

Managers need to measure performance for two very important reasons: (1) to evaluate performance relative to goals, and (2) to be able to control the process. But Lord Kelvin went further than that, saying that without measurement, we simply don't know what we're talking about. There was a government engineering agency that, over the years, had steadfastly refused to measure the performance of its major service. Given that engineering was its primary function, their reluctance was astonishing. Still, they were the sole provider of this service, so their business did not suffer. Given competition, we in industry do not have the luxury of ignoring the quality of our product. The customer will go elsewhere. We want to measure performance not only for the two reasons given above, but for a third: out of pride, so that we can proclaim to our customers and to our competition that we know what we are talking about.

Although referring to science, Lord Kelvin's remarks about measuring things are appropriate to industrial processes. But once we have decided to make measurements, a very large basket of questions is opened. What should be measured? How? When? We need to define what a measurement is. There is no universally recognized definition, but there are several that enjoy prominence, depending upon the field. Pedhazur (1991) offers a very simple definition, preeminent in the sociobehavioral sciences: "the assignment of numbers to aspects of objects or events according to one or another rule or convention." However, because we often use standards in quality, a definition quoted in Lamprecht (1993) is more to our point:

---
measurement

The quantitative determination of a physical magnitude by comparison with a fixed magnitude adopted as the standard, or by means of a calibrated instrument. The result of measurement is thus a numerical value expressing the ratio between the magnitude under examination and a standard magnitude regarded as a unit.

At first blush, this definition seems quite technical and precise, suggesting the measurement of a steel bar or an electronic frequency. But when you think about it, the definition is quite general. For example, it applies to measurements of uncertainty. There are products and services whose characteristics vary, so that statistical techniques are required in the measurement. Despite the uncertainty, we can make a quantitative determination of mean and variance of the quality. Shewart charts of product variation are one well-known technique of measuring process stability. The definition applies also to measurements of subjective performance. Customer evaluations such as "good," "fast," "important," and so on, can be perfectly valid measures of performance even though they are qualitative. There is often some confusion as to the difference between quality and quantity when speaking of measurement. Actually, the relationship is simple. Churchman and Ratoosh (1959) stress that quantities are measurements of qualities. In order that these evaluations be measurements, some sort of numerical scale must be associated with them.

Finally, the definition applies to fundamental business measurements such as profitability. We use various kinds of descriptive and predictive models in order to make business decisions. The outcome of these analyses is often the basis for making simple comparisons of alternatives. They are nevertheless measurements. Churchman and Ratoosh put it exactly right: "where a scientist seeks strong proofs, the business manager, faced with the need for making immediate decisions, is willing to settle for rules of thumb." Rules of thumb are coarse measurements, but they are valid if they follow measurement integrity. This book is aimed at a very broad readership, so discussion of specific measurements is beyond our bounds. Rather, in this chapter, we will discuss general considerations that ensure measurement integrity. They are often overlooked in the haste to start measuring, with a result that the measurements taken are invalid. These considerations are the components of measurement: objective, observability, parameters, methodology, metric, validity, parametric range, sensitivity, statistical analysis, instrumentation, test specifications, and standards.

Clearly, there is a lot more to measurement than just "doing it." And this is true even if you just want to make a simple measurement of whether the customer likes the service or not. For example, my pet peeve is to be in a restaurant with my mouth full of food, when the waiter comes up behind me and asks if everything is ok. The proprietor is conducting a simple measurement, perhaps not thinking much about how to do it. But involved in this poll are the following components, not well considered: objective, observability, parameter, methodology, metric, and standard. That's why I call these considerations the *components* of measurement, because they are there when you measure something whether you consider them or not. We will discuss these components in the following paragraphs.

GOVERNING COMPONENTS

Objective

As of this writing, the Congress of the United States has taken the habit to raise a hue and cry about our *objectives* before committing our troops to foreign entanglements. The reason for the commotion is that we have so often, in this century, gotten embroiled in endless morasses. Today's Congress pretends that by determining specific goals in advance, we can, at the appropriate time, declare victory and get out. This strategy hasn't worked in Washington because we never enunciate the real reasons why we commit troops. Nevertheless, the policy of determining objectives before you do anything in industry is a good one, and never more true than when you want to make a measurement.

Measurement is a non-value-added activity. That is not the same thing as saying it has no value. If the device being measured is unfit for service, then it had little value to begin with, so measurement may well save you both money and reputation. In this sense, measurement can have tremendous value. Begin by determining, in group session if necessary, why and what needs to be measured, in general terms. At this point in our consideration, we are thinking at the system level. How good is our product or service? Is the customer complaining about delivery delays? Why are there delays? Can it be the production process? Can it be the delivery process? Good and bad are always with respect to some criteria, but it makes both economic and engineering sense to keep measurement to a minimum. This is why so much thought has to be given to what ought to be measured, and which is why we have so many measurement considerations. Once we have decided that a measurement is required, the process of creating a measurement system begins, and we address its components one by one.

Validity

The purpose of measurement is to verify or validate some hypothesis. In Chapter 4, we used several questions posed by Boehm (1984) in order to distinguish between verification[1] and validity. Verification answers the question: "Are we doing things right?" Validation answers the question: "Are we doing the right things?" These questions give us an intuitive notion of verification and validation, but we need a deeper concept of them in order to make measurements.

Validity has two meanings with respect to measurement.[2] *Criterion Validity* means that the measurement allows prediction. There is a correlation between increases in the process and increases in the measurement. This kind of validity dictates what our measured parameters can be and what metric or measure of performance we can use. For example, the number of school days in the year is a valid criterion for measuring the quality of a school if there is a positive correlation between the number of days and the university acceptance rate of the school's graduates. The number of mechanics that work on your car is probably not a valid criterion for measuring the quality of the repair. *Construct validation* means the measurement allows extrapolation from an observed variable to an unobserved variable. For example, we measure engine temperature in our automobiles, but no longer measure oil pressure. We assume that if one is within tolerance, then so is the other. Construct validation in systems theory refers to conclusions about an inobservable state variable based upon an observance of an output variable, or conversely. We will talk more about this when we discuss observability.

Parameter

Once we've decided both the "goodness" of our product or service to be measured, and the system level at which we want to measure it, and bearing in mind the need for validity, we need to choose the parameter or parameters that we want to measure. By parameter, I mean the attribute of the object or event that we are going to measure. It may well be a quality characteristic, but it might also be a state variable if the two are not the same. Abraham and Ledolter (1983) say that the state of every system is described by two equations: a measurement equation and a system equation. This precision is too detailed for our purposes, but the concept is an important one that we discussed in Chapter 5 when we talked about state variables and product attributes. In sum, every dynamic process has characteristics or attributes that can be considered as variables. Some of them describe the state of the process. Some of them describe the quality of the product. Some of them can be seen; some cannot. Some are controllable; some are not. You must consider these issues in deciding what parameters to measure. In keeping with engineering, measurement variables are those that can be seen; state variables are those that describe the behavior of the system. The most effective attribute to measure is that in which the two sets are the same, but in general they are not.

Observability

In Chapter 1, we defined quality as "conformance to specifications," in which customer requirements are translated into physical dimensions. In other words, quality can be sensed and, therefore, measured. This is cold comfort, however, if the measurement reveals poor performance. The purpose of robust systems is to be able to control them to *improve* quality, so we are interested in making measurements for purposes of controlling the quality of the product. This introduces the notion of *observability*, an engineering concept. For robust systems, observability is related to controllability, which we defined heuristically in Chapter 5, and which is repeated below. Cadzow and Martens (1970) provide an heuristic definition of observability, presented side by side for comparison.

controllability

A system is *controllable* if it can be taken from any initial state to any desired state in finite time.

observability

A system is *observable* if it is possible to determine its present state from present and past values of the measured output variable.

What does all this mean to a manager? It means, quite simply, that it is important to relate the state variables of a production process to the quality characteristics that we want to enhance. The quality properties of our product are our output variables. Controllability allows us to adjust our system by adjusting its state. Observability allows us to adjust our system while measuring the quality characteristics, even though it is the state variables that we are changing. We must therefore know the exact dynamic relationship between the quality and state variables. A simple example is this: master chefs cooking on the range do not rely so much on the temperature of their heat as they do on observation of the dish that they are preparing. On the other hand, when cooking in the oven, they rely more on the state of the oven (determined by heat and time) than they do on observation. This choice of being able to control the process by measuring one or the other derives from their knowledge of the dynamic relationship between cooking

FIGURE 7–1

Observability with Respect to Three Subsystems

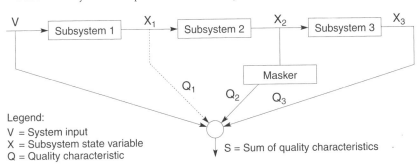

parameters and quality parameters, so that they can control the process by either.

The notion of observability is so important that we will call on a graphic to help us grasp the idea. In Figure 7–1, we have an industrial system with three dynamic subsystems. We'll make things easy on ourselves and assume that each process has a single mode, and that the modal behavior can be described by a single-state variable, X. By definition, we can measure all the quality characteristics, which we define as our outputs, Q. We measure them at point S, in the figure. We can also measure the state variables. The problem of observability is to relate the quality characteristics of the system to the state.

In Figure 7–1, the state variable X_3 and quality characteristic Q_3 are the same thing. For example, suppose subsystem 3 is the final station of a pump assembly, and the pump is being tested for its rated flow. We have selected flow rate as the state of that subsystem, and have decided that the flow rate also describes the quality of the pump, the faster the better. In this case, state and quality are the same; by measuring one we measure both, and either can be used as a control variable. It is also clear that the flow rate is the output of the pump, so in this example we have a happy coincidence of state, output, and quality.

We can measure quality characteristic Q_2 and state variable X_2, but we cannot see the direct relationship between them because of the masker. A masker is any process, filter, or device that obscures the relationship between the state variable and the output variable that is its end result. In our example situation, let the second subsystem be the insertion of a motor into the pump assembly. We decide that the state of the motor is defined by its revolutions per minute (RPM). There is no desired output to this subsystem, but we find that it has an inadvertent output: the speed of the motor generates a sound, and customers prefer quiet motors. Sound is therefore the quality characteristic Q_2, and the quieter the better. By generating calibration curves, we decide that it might be possible to relate, within limits, the state of the motor to its sound. If this works out over an acceptable range, then Q_2 can be used as a control variable.

Suppose that subsystem 1 is a variable transformer that steps up the input voltage to a driving voltage, X_1. Suppose, moreover, that the transformer generates heat and that customers have complained about burning themselves. Let Q_1 be the quality characteristic of heat. In our figure, there is no measurable relationship between the heat generated by the transformer and its voltage setting. The motor, too, causes heat. Q_1 cannot be used as a control variable because it cannot be related to any of the states. Subsystem 1 is not observable in an engineering sense.

We found in Chapter 5 that Federal Express was fortunate in being able to define its system state in terms of quality characteristics, that is, delivery times, pieces lost, and so on. On the other hand, in making products through chemical processes, it is usually necessary to use a number of precisely measured state variables in order to arrive at a single good quality characteristic. Obviously, the relationship of state to quality is complex. Every industry has its own decisions to make in deciding what parameters to measure in order to ensure quality. In choosing to measure a parameter, pick one that makes sense. If a parameter can serve as both state variable and quality characteristic, it is the first choice. Second choice goes to the parameters that have an isomorphic relationship between state and quality. This means that for each value of state there is a single value of quality, and conversely. Above all, bear in mind Gibson's warning (1990): Don't measure something just because it is easy to measure.

DESIGN COMPONENTS

Methodology

At this point in our measurement strategy, we're ready to decide on how to design our measurement program. There are two very basic ways to perform a measurement, one is static, the other dynamic. Which one we choose depends upon what we're looking for. A unit or process to be measured may have both fixed characteristics and characteristic ways of behaving. Characteristic behavior is called a mode. The measurement of a fixed characteristic is a static observation. The measurement of a mode is a dynamic observation. In order to delineate the two measurements, we will adopt some arbitrary definitions. An inspection is an observation of some fixed characteristic of the product or service. A test is an observation of a stimulus–response relation conducted over a finite time interval. The purpose of an inspection is to sense the *correctness* of a fixed characteristic of the product by comparing it to some standard. The purpose of a test is to establish the *correctness* of the behavior of the product relative to some standard. The rule of thumb is that if the product or service is dynamic, you must test it; if it is not, then an inspection may do. An inspection is not sufficient to determine the quality of a dynamic product because it does not examine modes.

The objectives of static and dynamic measurement are often confused. Nuances of confusion are shown in the following three examples. Continuity "tests" are an essential part of every electronic system test program. They are used to check the wiring between subsystems of the system, and are often called tests, but they are not. They are inspections. The system exists to do something, and continuity checks do not verify that something. By calling continuity checks "testing," the manufacturer may easily be led to believe that he has tested his product, and decide that continuity checks, therefore, represent a satisfactory test program.

The next two examples show how this wrong idea can be manifested. I once visited a manufacturer of industrial heaters and air conditioners. Although certain of its condensing units were designed to operate at 30 pounds per square inch (psi) of pressure, they were tested at only 5 psi. This kind of testing, although requiring an input, was essentially an inspection, and inadequate at that. It was essentially an inspection because it did not test the operational behavior of the compressor, and it was inadequate because it only verified the ability of the compressor to hold 5 psi, rather than its 30 psi requirement. As a final example, this same manufacturer produced vertical self-contained air conditioners. These systems contained complex assemblies of subsystems, and each was tested piecemeal. The modes of each subsystem were tested, but the system modes were not tested. There was no total system light-off or integration test. Thus, the test program did not include all appropriate levels of the system.

System verification was not achieved by this manufacturer. Testing is a complex subject that we will discuss in some detail in a later paragraph, but we can say here that it must be considered in terms of *verification:* The measurement of the correctness of a property or mode of a process over a domain of reference. The domain of reference is often a period of time, but it can be a range of any independent variable of interest.

It is important to retain generality in these considerations. The "system" can be a product as simple as a light switch (with two states: on and off), or it can be a far-flung logistics support process. The inspection or test can be observations of an inanimate object or interviews of personnel. In this book, all products, services, and systems are man-machine, which may affect the metric but not the method.

Statistical Analysis

Statistical analysis is often considered a method of measurement, but strictly speaking, it is not. Statistics is simply making sense out of data. Measurement supplies the data. If the data have no meaning, then we wind up with GIGO (garbage in, garbage out). This is not always easy to see because statistical analysis *will* make sense out of the data. But this sense may be about the numbers and not about the thing measured. This is why the methodology of measurement is a discipline in itself. If you are going to measure something that hasn't been measured before, you will probably need professional consulting. It would be wise to use it anyway. Still, statistical methods are such a major component of measurement of both on-line and off-line processes that Chapter 8 is devoted entirely to it.

Metrics

A metric is the unit used as a measure of performance. Feet, centimeters, pounds, errors per line of code, furlongs per fortnight, rating, score—all are metrics. A metric may be nominal, ordinal, or cardinal. A nominal metric assigns numbers to the parameter being measured. An ordinal metric assigns a relation or preference order to the measured parameter. There is no indication of strength of preference; to say that customers prefer product x to product y may be a valid measurement, but it doesn't say *how much* they prefer x to y. A cardinal metric assigns a relation order to the measured parameter and also provides strength to the relation. A Richter scale is a good example of a cardinal measure. We know not only that an earthquake of 5.0 is more violent than one of 4.0, but we also know that it is 10 times more violent.

Rose (1995) lists several attributes that good metrics must have. They should provide value to customers, they should be linked to company goals, and they should provide information over time. In this way the metrics describe instant and trend dynamics. An additional attribute is this: where possible, a noninterfering metric should be used, one that does not influence the parameter being measured. This is not always possible; in fact, the metrics used in destructive testing clearly impact the parameter. If we are measuring the packing strength of a box, then the metric might be "pounds per square inch at which the box breaks." On the other hand, choosing a metric to measure worker performance must be done with care, lest the measurement be demoralizing. Deming frequently talked against instilling fear in the workforce, and it is often the metric that does it.

Metrics can be subjective. For example, we might ask management to rank the importance of quality in the various departments or activities of their company. We would provide them with a scale, say, one for not important and ten for maximum importance. Intuitively, we can see that there is little that is scientific in this measurement. We are asking for pure opinion. However, it can be made scientific by introducing randomness and large numbers in the sampling, by choosing experts in the evaluation, and by applying criteria of validity and reliability in the measurement program. A cardinal scale can be derived for this measurement that would be acceptable to science; sociobehavioral scientists do this often.

Metrics can be objective, but this does not ensure the validity of the measurement. This is particularly true if the process being measured is uncertain. Most of the well-known statistical methods are based on the idea of independence between samples and the law of large numbers.[3] The methods may be invalid for a given production line with serial dependence or small volume. You may count the number of customers who are attracted to a certain product, and if you have a good idea of the total population to whom it is available, then you can come up with a hard number in terms of market draw. But if your product is for the general market, then you may really need to look at the *kinds* of customers that you are attracting with it. In this case, the metric is simple—a pure count. But the method may not be valid.

Range

The range of a measurement can refer to several things, but I speak of it here as a measurement control. To clarify this idea, consider several kinds of measurement in which range occurs. In control charting, the variation in the measurement of an attribute that occurs from object to object on the production line is called range. Analogous to variance, range is properly a statistical consideration.

Alternatively, the range of a measurement may refer to the extent of it. For example, the range of a poll may be all adult males living in Minnesota. The range of a measurement may be the ability of a group of employees to lift and carry 50 to 100 pounds. A measurement may require a stimulus-response, where we vary the input over a set of its values while observing a set of the output values. In this case, the set of values over which the input is varied is called the measurement *domain,* and the set of resultant output values is the measurement *range.* For example, a chef may vary the oven broiling time from 15 to 25 minutes (the domain) to achieve rare, medium, and well-done steaks (the range). In designing an experiment, we need to delineate in our own minds range as variation and range as a measurement control.

The range of a measurement is also a factor in its validity. This is clearly true in the sociobehavioral sciences; every book on the subject talks about range restriction. But it is also true of every kind of measurement, even the most ordinary. For example, most gasoline gauges read from empty to full, but accurate measurement is only along the middle of the range. As you get down at the low end, where you are *really* concerned about accuracy, the measurement is quite imprecise. This is why Toyota introduced the nonlinear gauge in its *Camry* model some years ago. The gauge is quite accurate at the lower 25 percent level. However, the nonlinear scale proved to be disconcerting to many customers. Sometimes you win the battles and lose the wars.

Suppose that you want to measure the voltage of the battery in your smoke alarm, nominally nine volts. A meter that reads in the range of 20 to 50 volts will not do, but a meter reading in the range of 0 to 1,000 volts will not do either. In the scale of 0 to 1,000, nine is down at the nonlinear range of the meter, at which it is relatively imprecise. Since a battery that reads even eight volts may be too weak to drive the alarm, you are asking a meter that can read to 1,000 volts to distinguish accurately a one-volt differential.

Sensitivity

Variation is often found in the results of a measurement, due to the dynamic or random nature of the attribute being measured, or to the environment, or to the measurement itself. Sensitivity refers to the ability of the measurement to cope with variation, and because of this, is sometimes confused with the precision of the measurement. Moreover, precision is often confused with accuracy, so that we need to clarify these ideas in order to understand sensitivity.

The accuracy of a measurement is its agreement with the standard to which it is compared. For example, if the standard is one volt, then a measurement of 0.99 volts is more accurate than one of 1.10 volts. The precision of a measurement is the agreement, time after time, of the results of the same measurement. A number of measurements of the same attribute or a number of runs of the same experiment must be conducted in order to determine precision. A series of measurements of low variance is more precise than a series of high variance. Thus, a series of measurements that has little variation is properly called *precise* rather than *sensitive*. Within the context of variation, sensitivity is more appropriate to the instrumentation used, and is discussed in the next section.

Measurement usually contains some error. The error may be due to the measuring system itself or it may be due to random variation in the attribute that is being measured. The measurement results in data. If small errors in data cause big changes in our results or conclusions, then the measurements have little practical value. Determining the effect of small errors on the results of an experiment or measurement is called sensitivity analysis. Thus, the sensitivity of a measurement refers to the relationship between the measurement conditions, parametric or environmental. A measurement of low sensitivity means that the results are relatively "insensitive" to small environmental or parametric changes.

Instrumentation

We have discussed some of the problems inherent in measurement validity, particularly in the arena of sociobehavioral measurement. When it comes to measuring a physical characteristic, the validity of the measurement depends as well upon the instruments that are used. The instrumentation used must have the appropriate parametric range, accuracy, sensitivity, and calibration. By parametric range is meant that the instrument can cover the domain or range of the measured variable over its linear capability. Accuracy needs little explanation, except that more is not necessarily better. Accuracy is expensive, so you need to determine and meet the requirements.

Sensitivity is a measure of the degree of dependence of one quantity upon the value of another quantity. This is often interpreted as the effect upon one quantity of a *change* in the value of another quantity. In measuring with instruments, we use the term to refer to the ability of an instrument to detect small variation in the measured unit, changes in temperature, viscosity, or pH, for example. Sensitivity is particularly important if the measurement is being made for closed loop control because compensating action may be needed quickly to prevent or arrest the manufacture of bad product.

The dynamic operation of any equipment is established by the manufacturer in making adjustments of variables, gains, and power within the unit. These adjustments establish the accuracy, scale factors, and linearity of the equipment. With time, minute wear and tear occurs in the equipment, entailing readjustment to restore its operational characteristics. This is called calibration. We usually do not wait for equipment to be obviously wrong, but schedule calibration periodically. Sometimes it's the law. We have all noted the calibration stickers on gasoline pumps, which are required by law in many states to be achieved annually. A measurement made with an uncalibrated instrument is questionable, and may be legally worthless.

Specifications and Standards

In measurement, specifications provide the detailed technical requirements that ensure verification and validation. As a general rule, the more specific the technical description or requirement, the more costly is the measurement. There are, of course, exceptions. In measurements that utilize models, specification error refers to the correctness of the theoretical model. Specifications are often defined in terms of upper and lower limits, in recognition that infinite precision is not possible. A good deal of thought is needed in determining these limits, along with recognition that they may have to be changed. For example, we may specify that a cylinder should be three inches in diameter, ± 0.001 inch, only to discover that our production system cannot consistently meet these "specs." Very often, a certain amount of Kentucky windage (intuition) goes into specifications. If the production system is not capable, there are only two choices: widen the specs or buy a new production system.

Standards provide uniformity in the conduct of the measurement. They allow the same measurement to be made of the same parameter irrespective of place, time, or conditions. In some cases, a standard is a procedure. In others, it is a physical property such as a 1-ohm resistor or the wavelength of a radioactive element. We sometimes speak of standards of behavior. Since measurement is defined in terms of comparison to a standard, there can be no measurement without one. Quality performance requires standards throughout the organization.

SYSTEM TESTING

System testing is a special approach to the methodology of measurement. *Methodology* differs from *method* by the suffix *ology*, from **logos**—reasoning. There is a great deal of thought that goes into testing a system. Because a system is an assembly of parts or functions, we measure its performance differently from the way we measure the parts or functions themselves. A system exists for a synergistic purpose and this purpose must be measured. That is why we said that a system should be tested under its operating conditions. The test must have integrity. *A system test has integrity if it is comprehensive, continuous, and complete.* A test with integrity describes the system condition. If the criteria are not met, then the condition of the system is in doubt.

Comprehensive System Test

A test is comprehensive if all modes of the system are tested, including intermodal testing, where intermode operation is one of the system specifications. A simple example of cross-modal operation takes place during medical surgery. In addition to the biological system under the knife, the respiratory and cardiac systems are also monitored, and as one impacts the other, remedial action is taken. Constant measurement of the various subsystems is required. Another example of interactive modes is that of a home facsimile machine. Mine has three modes: manual, automatic, and answering machine. No matter what the mode, either the telephone handset or the facsimile capability is on line.

There are many examples of systems that are not particularly effective in their operations. A quick example is the local supermarket. It usually has two modes of operation: regular and express. We find that we often choose our supermarket based upon how well they operate both modes. Every day is a test, and the market that concentrates on one mode and neglects the other fails its comprehensiveness, and probably loses customers to boot. Then, of course, there are cases where we may not want intermodal testing, or even multiple mode testing. The automobile is a complex system, but when you take it to the garage for a tune-up, that may be all you want to pay for. There is nothing wrong with limited testing, but it is not system testing.

F I G U R E   7–2

Intermodal Action Requiring Comprehensiveness in System Testing

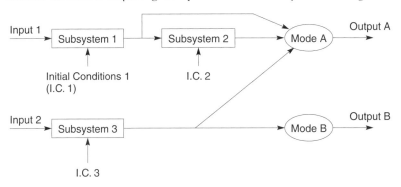

The system shown in Figure 7–2 demonstrates why comprehensiveness is needed for test integrity. The system has three subsystems and two modes of behavior. Mode A can be stimulated by any of the three subsystems. It is not possible to tell the cause from the effect, nor is the system comprehensively tested by a simple verification of each mode. From the diagram, it will take at least four experiments to verify the system.

Continuous System Test

Dynamic system tests can run a long time. Several hours is not unusual; some Department of Defense tests take several days. It may be necessary to stop during the test either because the experiment is too long or because a system failure requires troubleshooting. This creates a de facto segmented test. There are strong engineering and mathematical criteria related to continuity in dynamic system testing. Basically, they require that the system state transit from its initial state to a final state (1) uninterrupted; or (2) if the test is interrupted, the modes or subsystems of the preceding segment must be independent of the modes or subsystems of the following segment; or (3) if the test is interrupted, the initial state of the following segment must match the final state of the preceding segment. These criteria ensure the validity of the test.

These criteria are not as easy to follow as they may appear. Because a large system test may involve a dozen or more players and perhaps several hours or more, it is very difficult to run an uninterrupted system level test. Criteria 1 and 2 are both approached the same way—in the design of the test itself. System tests should be designed in independent segments. The beginning of each segment should contain *initialization,* that is, the set-up of all initial conditions to establish the system's initial state for that segment.[4]

Criterion 3 is extraordinarily difficult to meet for most dynamic systems. The difficulty is in recreating the state at the instant before interruption. Generally, if a system test segment is interrupted for some reason, it is best to restart the test by initialization and rerun the entire segment. This issue is less important in the test of stochastic systems, where system state can seldom be duplicated anyway. The objective of stochastic systems tests is less often to verify a system state trajectory than to verify the state distribution.

Completion

Some people often say that a test is complete when the last step is done. This sounds good, but I have seen system testing arrive at the end with a series of alibis.[5] Often the testing agency and the customer have different objectives. For example, a ship repair yard will have extensive system testing to do, which is achieved by accomplishing a series of various level tests. Since each test represents a work item or subset of a work item, the objective of the shipyard is to complete the work items. However, the objective of the ship's force is to be able to go in harm's way. The two objectives are not the same. A system test is complete if the assigned state boundary conditions are achieved. Always look at the system state. Measure the state.

It seems like slovenly test policy to waive system test criteria on the basis of an alibi, but lest we be too harsh in our judgment, we must all admit that we sometimes do the same thing. We take our car to the garage for a diagnostic test and the repairman says that, in his opinion, the frammis will go out within the next 1,000 miles. Well, how much is a new frammis? $750? One test criterion waived instantly.

IMPLEMENTATION

Hardly anyone goes overboard on measurement. The reason is that it costs money. As I said earlier, it is not a value-added activity. So, few of us need to be cautioned about overdoing it. But we *do* need to be cautioned to do enough. Every process must be measured because measurement supplies the data required for control, and control is required for robustness. Although we are not likely to do too much measurement, it is possible to do a lot of *dumb* measurement, lacking reason. We can avoid this on our own by developing a well-thought-out measurement policy. This policy can be developed by addressing the measurement components, beginning with determining the objectives of measurement for each process. These components compose the structure of implementation.

There are two big costs that must be faced up front. The first is knowledge; the second is plant. Without knowledge we will make *ignorant* measurements, lacking specific technical know-how. We often cannot avoid this on our own, because measurement is a field in itself. Statistical measurement even more so. For example, if you have stochastic processes of low volume or of unknown distribution, what kind of valid measurements can you make? Can you do control charting? The cost of knowledge includes training persons to measure their own output, and it may mean the hiring of engineers, statisticians, and technicians just to do measurement activities and perhaps provide training.

By plant is meant staff, equipment, laboratories, and shops. Measurement can require an extensive plant, depending upon the nature of the company's operations. The composition of calibration and metrology labs depends upon the business of concern, but we will discuss guidelines of their operation, as well as building the general measurement structure.

Inspection and Testing

Measurement is the gathering of certain kinds of data. You gather these data by observation, through a system of inspection or testing. These activities are conducted at general stages of a production process: receiving, in-process, and final. Inspections should be performed by the persons who did the value-added activity that is being inspected, because each person is responsible for his own quality control. Testing is more complicated and dedicated test personnel might be required, particularly at the final stage where the product is likely to have system characteristics.

Figure 7–3 depicts a typical inspection and test arrangement for a production process organized as a workstation sequence. A workstation is a place and time in which an activity occurs. Examples of relevant activity are work, inspection, measurement, and decision. Because there are 43 workstations in this particular process, identifying each of them would complicate the picture and add little to a general view of the process itself. Therefore, the activities are grouped into functional subsystems, each displayed as a block in the figure. The location of inspection and repair stations and test points is only partly dictated by the technical process itself. If there is statistical dependence between the workstations, which is the general case, then the effects of serial dependence decrease the process reliability, so that this, too, should be a consideration in the location of inspection points.

Although Figure 7–3 depicts an assembly line, it must be viewed in a completely general sense. For example, a software development process would be quite similar. In this case, inspections would include reviews and walk-throughs. Tests would be both white box (structure) and black box (functional). The comments we made about locating these inspection and test points in the assembly line process remain valid for software processes also, as well as any production or service system.

Inspection and Test Records

Records contribute to process control because they represent corporate memory of the dynamics of quality and reliability. Often, the raw data ends up in a vault. This may be a necessary evil, but before the data go into the vault, quality, reliability, and maintainability analysis should be performed, not only to determine present status, but also to indicate trends and equipment and process life cycles. We need to bear in mind why we make measurements in the first place. Analytical results should be graphic and automated, available at a moment's notice.

F I G U R E   7–3

A Workstation Sequence with Inspection and Test Sites

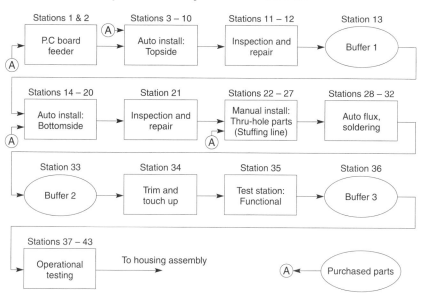

Records of inspection and testing should be maintained for other reasons also. We mentioned inspection of incoming product. Suppose that a company has a policy of acceptance sampling, but in some cases finds it necessary to waive inspection, perhaps for urgent production purposes. If an incoming product is released on a waiver, it must be identified and recorded in order to permit immediate recall in the event of nonconformance. This is certainly true of chemical and pharmaceutical processes, but is a good idea in any industry.

On the subject of outcome, inspection and test status of product should be identified with tags or labels, records or test software. In this way, records demonstrate that only product that has passed the required inspections and tests is used in installation or is delivered to the customer. In every process, there should be quality procedures that define and describe the company inspection and test requirements. Procedures *on station* ensure operator consistency, a necessary element in control and robustness.

Calibration and Metrology Equipment

Test equipment to be used in measuring, inspection, or testing, must be maintained in calibration in order to provide valid data. The very nature of calibration implies the need of associated calibration procedures and records. On the other hand, concentrating on calibration can miss the big picture; it is only a subset of metrology. For example, some industries do not manufacture a product measurable by a machine; subjective judgments are required. Even here, it is useful to maintain records of ordinal reference. In this case, the subjective standard used becomes the calibrating standard. There is no substitute for thought. There are commonly recognized criteria in determining the what, when, and how of measurement. First, we must identify the measurements to be made and the accuracy needed to make them. Then we must select appropriate equipment. A calibration program must be defined for the measuring equipment. This program will include procedures and schedules, the former to account for the complexity of the measurement or equipment, the latter because accuracy tends to drift with time.

Control of Nonconforming Product

The integrity of the company's inspection and test process is reflected by how it controls nonconforming product. Two examples show why. In the first, a purchased part fails acceptance testing or receipt inspection, yet is urgently needed for production. This case was mentioned in discussing the need to keep records. If records are kept and the part meticulously identified, then it can be tracked and recalled at a later date if necessary. The second example is when a product fails final inspection or test, but the customer agrees to accept it by concession. This case was mentioned in discussing the notion of test completion. Establishing procedures for, and keeping records of nonconforming product ensure realistic customer expectations. Finally, control can reduce inventory. By establishing policies and procedures, you get a grip on the problem and are less prone to regrading or reclassifying an inferior product. An unplanned inventory of reclassified product essentially puts a company into another, less rewarding market.

FIGURE 7–4

A General Schematic for Corrective Action and the Control of
Nonconforming Product

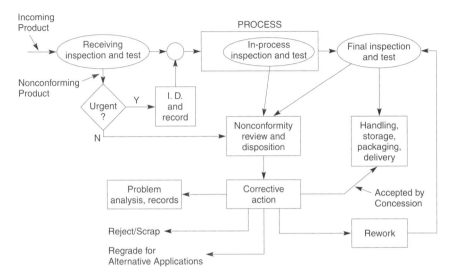

Corrective Action

The inspection and test process is designed to reduce the release
of nonconforming product. Several alternatives are available for
such disposition, and a general diagram of the whole process is
shown in Figure 7–4. The corrective action may be rework, regrade
of product for alternate application, reject, issue to the customer
by concession, or other disposition. Usually it is not difficult to
determine the reasonable thing to do. One company produces
printed circuit cards that have an end-of-line value of $60 or more.
Obviously, rework is a far better alternative than scrap, and they
have developed an efficient repair process for this purpose. Other
companies apparently do not put a great deal of thought into the
matter. As we mentioned, some companies do not admit to nonconformity and regrade or reclassify product as a viable alternative to improving the quality of their premier process. This secondary inventory competes with the top of the line and so adds
complexity to the cost of poor quality. Other companies do not
distinguish between nonconformities discovered internally and

those discovered after delivery, although clearly the latter can be expensive, both in actual cash outlay and in terms of customer dissatisfaction. I know of one company that maintains a sizable staff of field technicians for warranty work. Pareto analysis of failure data revealed that the major contributor to warranty work was wiring failure. The nature of wiring leads me to suspect that the failures existed before the product went out the door, and could have been found by better test procedures. Repairing wiring mistakes is relatively inexpensive if found in the factory, and dirt cheap if found right away. It stands to reason that if the factory is in San Diego and the customer is in Chicago, then the cost of failing to find the defect before delivery is going to be expensive.

An idea of the cost of quality is indicated in Figure 7–5 for two very disparate industries. It is clear that costs increase greatly the longer in process time that the nonconformity stays uncorrected. At first blush the software industry seems to have a modest rise, but this is because of the logarithmic ordinate scale. In fact, both costs rise exponentially, and we can infer that for most industries the cost of quality has a generally steep slope with respect to time. Clearly, the lesson to be learned is to adopt policies and timely procedures for corrective action.

Audit

Inspection and testing are *quality control* functions and should reside within the productive processes themselves. Auditing is a different story. A quality assurance audit is a systematic examination of representative aspects of quality systems within an organization, its suppliers, and how it manages its customer requirements. At the beginning of this chapter, we offered several definitions of measurement, one of which is "the assignment of numbers to aspects of objects or events according to one or another rule or convention." In this perspective, we may consider that auditing is measurement. Its purpose is to distinguish form and substance. A complete measurement program should then include inspection and test processes, and an internal audit organization. But the audit group must be independent of the processes that it audits, so that it should be part of the *quality assurance* function, and external to the production processes.

F I G U R E   7–5

The Cost of Quality in Two Disparate Industries, Relative to the Time in Process in Which Fault Is Detected

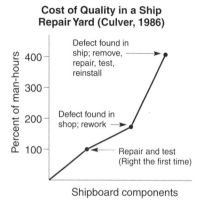

Cost of Quality in a Ship Repair Yard (Culver, 1986)

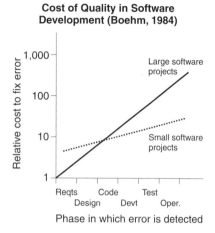

Cost of Quality in Software Development (Boehm, 1984)

(However, a recommendation for a quality assurance *function* is not a recommendation for a quality assurance *department*. The two are not necessarily the same.)

In sum, robustness requires control, and control requires measurement. Substantive things can be measured, often objectively, perhaps nonparametrically. In keeping with Lord Kelvin, we know about them only to the extent we measure them. Measurement is a discipline in itself, requiring extensive knowledge about metrology as well as about the processes being measured. Even more than that, effective measurement of dynamic organizations requires a program of goals, policies, and procedures.

Most production and service systems are stochastic processes. If measurements are to be made, then statistical methods are essential. We address this issue in the next chapter.

N O T E S

1. **Verification.** The Latin origin of this word is *verus,* meaning truth. Many disciplines define verification in terms appropriate to the field, but they all come down to the Latin origin. In software engineering,

for example, Boehm (1984) defines verification thus: given some objective criteria, one can answer true or false. In the same field, Deutsch (1982) defines it as an activity that ensures that each step of the development process correctly echoes the intentions of the immediately preceding step. Law and Kelton (1991) say that verification is determining that a simulation computer program performs as intended. If a fixed characteristic resembles its standard, it has been verified. If a process mode resembles its standard over the domain of reference, it is verified. Thus, both inspection and test methods verify. Testing is performed over some variation of a reference or independent variable; hence, verification contains not one sample, but many.

2. **Validation.** Pedhazur, for example, identifies a widely used tripartite of validity: content, construct, and criterion. However, he considers content as an inherent component of construct validity, and states that the chief reason that content validity has gained prominence is that the government stresses content validity in determining achievement. Ghiselli et al. (1981) define *content validity* of a set of measurement operations as the degree to which the set measures the desired characteristics as judged from the appropriate content of the operations. These authors, too, agree that content validity becomes a part of construct validity if experts judge the adequacy of the methods used to sample the content from the universe of content. In perusing the material in the field, one is struck by references to many different kinds of validity, but Pedhazur admits that the whole subject is debatable in the sociobehavioral sciences. Some savants insist that there is only one kind of validity. Others insist that there are many. It may be safer to say that a measurement is either valid or not, depending upon many or several criteria. Pedhazur tries to avoid implying that there are different types of validity, preferring to talk of inferential and evidential validation processes. Hence, construct and criterion.

3. **Randomness, Independence, and the Law of Large Numbers.** Events with uncertain outcome or processes having uncertain behavior are called random. The stock market is an example of random behavior. Random events or variables that behave without mutual influence are independent, and this independence greatly simplifies the analysis of their behavior. Sometimes sequential random events are not independent, but become independent with time. Suppose that we sample a random event, say the price of IBM stock on Monday. That price is a random variable. Then we sample the price again on Tuesday. That price too, is a random variable. Are the two independent? Perhaps not. But if we allow enough time between our samples, we may find that the second sample is independent of the first as time has eroded

influence. It takes system expertise to determine the interdependence of system parameters. The law of large numbers says that the more samples we take, the more closely our estimate of the population mean will approximate the true population mean.

4. **Initialization.** At first blush this appears to be one of those awful words created by people with little regard for English. Perhaps it is. Yet, within the confines of the engineering world it carries a meaning that is not captured by *beginning, start,* or *initiation.* If you stop a test for any reason, then begin it again at some later time irrespective of system conditions, you have started or begun the test again, or initiated testing, if you will. But that is not initialization. *Initialization* has a specific meaning: to begin a test at the beginning of a segment of that test at which system initial conditions for that segment have been set. When the Test Conductor gives the command to initialize, all testing personnel set their initial conditions *first,* then commence testing.

5. **Alibi.** In test engineering, the term *alibi* does not have the negative connotation that it suffers in popular language. It is simply a reason, valid or not, for a failure in the test. You seldom know, before troubleshooting, why a failure occurs. The search for a failure is partly objective and partly subjective. The subjective part is the alibi. Alibis are often based in experience and they can get you started in the right direction. The problem with them is that they are sometimes assumed to be correct assessments, and on the basis of this assumption, the test is continued with the promise of repairing or replacing the failed part at some later time. But until the failed part is replaced and the test successfully rerun, we can never be sure of the cause. In a test with integrity, an alibi may absolutely not be used to waive a criterion, but it would be naïve to believe that this event is rare.

REFERENCES

Abraham, Bovas, and Johannes Ledolter. *Statistical Methods for Forecasting.* New York: John Wiley & Sons, 1983.

Boehm, Barry W. "Verifying and Validating Software Requirements and Design Specifications." *IEEE Transactions, Software Engineering,* January 1984, pp. 75–83.

Cadzow, James A., and Hinrich R. Martens. *Discrete-Time and Computer Control Systems.* Englewood Cliffs, NJ: Prentice Hall, 1970.

Churchman, C. West, and Philburn Ratoosh. *Measurement: Definitions and Theories.* New York: John Wiley & Sons, 1959.

Culver, John A., Capt., USN. "Ship Overhauls and Quality Assurance in Private Shipyards." *Naval Engineers Journal,* January, 1986, pp. 46–58.

Deming, W. Edwards. *Out of the Crisis.* Cambridge, MA: The Center for Advanced Engineering Study, Massachusetts Institute of Technology, 1991.

Deutsch, Michael S. *Software Verification and Validation: Realistic Project Approaches.* Englewood Cliffs, NJ: Prentice Hall, 1982.

Ghiselli, Edwin E.; John P. Campbell; and Sheldon Zedeck. *Measurement Theory for the Behavioral Sciences.* San Francisco: W. H. Freeman & Company, 1981.

Gibson, John E. *How to Do Systems Analysis.* Englewood Cliffs, NJ: Prentice Hall (in review).

Lamprecht, James L. *Implementing the ISO 9000 Series.* New York: Marcel Dekker, Inc., 1993. Reprinted by courtesy of Marcel Dekker, Inc.

Law, Averill M., and W. David Kelton. *Simulation, Modeling, and Analysis.* New York: McGraw-Hill, 1991.

Pedhazur, Elazar, and Liora Pedhazur-Schmelkin. *Measurement, Design, and Analysis: An Integrated Approach.* Hillsdale, NJ: Lawrence Erlbaum Associates, 1991.

Rose, Kenneth H. "A Performance Measurement Model." *Quality Progress,* February 1995, pp. 63–66.

Stimson, William A. "Principles of Systems Testing." *Naval Engineers Journal,* November 1988, pp. 48–58.

Thomson, William (Lord Kelvin). *Popular Lectures and Addresses.* Vol. 1, 2nd ed. London: MacMillen, 1891.

8

⑥ STATISTICAL MEASUREMENT

STATISTICS

Measured quality of a manufactured product is always subject to a certain amount of variation as a result of chance. Some stable system of chance causes is inherent in any particular scheme of production and inspection. Variation within this stable pattern is inevitable. The reasons for variation outside this stable pattern may be discovered and corrected.

Walter A. Shewart, 1931

We usually make measurements by taking data. If there is a random element in the data, then statistics can make sense out of it. Almost everything that might interest a manufacturer has a random nature, from the production line to the marketplace. Sourcing, inventory, production, and demand are all subject to uncertainty. As Shewart points out, quality characteristics have variation. Although he was referring to manufactured product, Deming and others have firmly established that the quality characteristics of services have variation also, so that the measurement of every process in the corporation is likely to require statistical analysis.

Some of the techniques of statistics are conveniently called *off-line statistical measurements.* Ones that we will discuss are parameter estimation, tests of hypotheses, analysis of variance, and regression analysis. These methods are often used to make measurements in a wide variety of activities such as product design, production engineering, service design, and the socio-behavioral sciences. Some of the techniques are conveniently called *on-line statistical measurements.* The most common ones are control charting and acceptance sampling. These methods are not only effective in production or service operation, but have been shown to be applicable to a wide description of human activity. For example, a manager can control chart the performance of his employees to determine their ability as a group. This shows the upper and lower limits inherent in that group and points the finger for improvement on training rather than on blame for a given individual.

Regression analysis was discussed briefly in Chapter 5 because of its role in process design. Nevertheless, its fundamental action is to measure something and it is widely used in both technical and social fields, so it is discussed in a little more detail in this chapter.

In this chapter we introduce some techniques used in measurement, but we need to begin with a few notions about statistics in general. We shall assume a process, of whatever function, whose output has some random variation in a characteristic or quality that is important to us and that we want to measure. By random variation, I mean that the characteristic has one value one time, and another value another time, each with a certain probability. The set of all values that it takes on, with their associated probabilities, is called a *distribution,* or *population.* The two terms are often interchanged.

It may not be feasible to measure all the values. If we had a group of about 20 people, we could measure their height, for example. Then we could determine exactly the average height and variation of that group, or population. However, if we had 10,000 people, measuring them all would not be feasible. Instead, we would take samples, then use the power of statistics to make judgments of the population based on the samples. A *sample* is a subset of data from the population, and is called, naturally enough, the sample distribution. If you make reference to a sample population, then the population it comes from is called the *parent.*

A population has two parameters of frequent interest: the *average* value and its *variance.* We don't usually refer to a parameter when speaking of sample populations, but use the word *statistic,* which is a measure on a sample. Average values can be expressed as mean, median, and mode, and all three are used in one kind of analysis or another. However, in this book we are interested only in the characteristic quality of things and need only one type of average for demonstrative purposes. So to simplify matters, we will use the mean value in all our demonstrations. Variance is a pre-empted term in statistics. It refers to the dispersion of data about the average value. Its square root is called a *standard deviation,* a term that may be more familiar to some readers than variance because of its frequent use in the socio-behavioral sciences. Finally, a *statistical inference* is a decision, estimate, prediction, or generalization about the population based on the sample.

OFF-LINE MEASUREMENT

Parameter Estimation

A population has many parameters that characterize it, but most of them are of interest only to statisticians. As we mentioned, the two parameters of general interest are the average value and the variance. Because sampling is not free, a sample population will usually be smaller than the parent, perhaps much smaller. For example, a political poll will contain only a few thousand samples from the voter population of many millions. The purpose of the sample is to get some idea of the mean and variance of the parent based upon the statistics of the sample. There are rules for estimation to ensure its validity. The estimate will never be exact, but it can be arbitrarily close to the parent parameter if we use good estimators, and moreover, we can determine a confidence interval in our estimate.

The technique that we use to make an estimate is called an *estimator.* A good estimator has four important properties: non-bias, consistency, sufficiency, and relative efficiency. An estimate is unbiased if the expected value of the estimator is equal to the true parameter. An estimator is consistent if the probability that the estimate is close to the true parameter is greater for larger samples than for smaller ones. A statistic is a sufficient estimator if it uses all the information in the data that are relevant to the true value. Relative efficiency refers to the standard error of the estimate found in two different estimators, the estimator with the smallest error being the most efficient.

Tests of Hypotheses

Suppose that we conjecture about something, an idea that if this happened, that would follow. A hypothesis is a conjecture put in the form of an assumption that can be tested. For example, we might conjecture that if they had fought, Rocky Marciano would have beaten Muhammed Ali. This idea is not a hypothesis because it cannot be tested. On the other hand, suppose we conjecture that a wine might improve if given some time. Then we define conditions about its storage, assume that it will or will not improve (the hypothesis), and carry out the test. By convention, the hypothesis that it will *not* improve is called the *null hypothesis*; the hypothesis that it will improve is called the *alternate hypothesis.* Also by convention, it is the null hypothesis that must be proven.

A statistical hypothesis is a conjecture about the distribution of a random variable. We want to know if the hypothesis that we have made is true or false, and we do that on the basis of sampling. The hypothesis is about the distribution, not about the sample. Hypothesis testing compares two values of a parameter, each representing a distinct, mutually exclusive proposition. For example, suppose that we intend to make a change to a process and want to know whether there will be a resultant change in some aspect of the process. Consider the following example.

We have a chemical process whose yield varies according to a normal distribution, as shown on the left in Figure 8–1. Through experience we know the average value and the variance of this distribution. We want to improve the yield and think that we can do it by changing a factor of the process. We don't have permission to test the new change over a long period of time, but must come to a rather quick judgment about its improvement with hypothesis testing.

The change is made. The changed process will also vary its yield and we take samples to detect the improvement, if any. Whether there was an improvement or not is resolved by posing two hypotheses. The null hypothesis is that no change in the yield average has occurred. The alternate hypothesis is that the average yield has increased. If sampling the changed process provides statistics that indicate the alternate distribution shown on the right in Figure 8–1, then we easily arrive at a verification of improvement.

F I G U R E   8–1

Two Distributions of an Average Yield, Indicating an Original Distribution and an Estimated Distribution Based upon Sampling a Changed Process

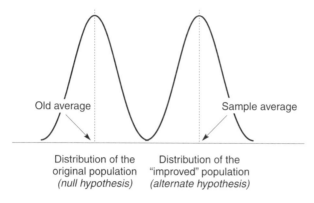

Old average   Sample average

Distribution of the   Distribution of the
original population   "improved" population
(null hypothesis)   *(alternate hypothesis)*

Our new average is so much greater than the previous one that, even given the variance, the process is clearly improved. We have succeeded in shifting the entire distribution to improved values of the yield.

In general, though, no such luck obtains. Usually, improvement or change is incremental, as indicated in Figure 8–2. Here, the sample average yield is higher than the old yield, but given the same variance, we see a great deal of overlap between the distributions of the two hypotheses. For very high increases in yield, clearly improvement is demonstrated. We obtain yields never before achieved. But for a large range of samples the picture is not so clear. We cannot be sure if a new distribution even exists. For example, if our sample average is in the range of yield values called *alpha region,* the conclusions are ambiguous. Yes, the sample average from the alpha region might come from a newly created distribution, or it might simply be in the higher end of the old distribution.

This dilemma is resolved by dividing the distribution of the old process into acceptance and rejection regions. Consider Figure 8–2 again. The area under a normal curve denotes the probability that a particular yield will obtain. So we go out along the right "tail" of the old distribution to a yield value where the area under the curve to its left is 95 percent of the total area. We denote this

F I G U R E   8–2

Ambiguous Regions of a Test of Hypotheses

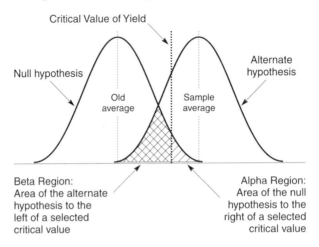

yield as the *critical value* of yield. Any sample yield higher than that has only a 5 percent chance of being in the old distribution. We are satisfied with a 95 percent assurance of success and call the small area to the right of the critical value the alpha region.

Recall that we must prove the null hypothesis. Thus, if a sample yield is in the alpha region or higher, we reject the null hypothesis and accept the alternate. For this reason, the alpha region is called the *rejection region* of the null hypothesis. A sample yield lower in value than the critical value therefore falls into the *acceptance region* of the null hypothesis. We can choose different values of yield to represent the critical value, depending upon the confidence level that we want. For example, we could pick an alpha region of 2.5 percent, implying that we want to be very sure our new process is better. Conversely, we could pick an alpha region of 10 percent, implying that we will accept a less conclusive result.

Since we are dealing in probability, it is possible to commit two types of error in our conclusions based upon the hypotheses: (1) The sample average can occur in the rejection region and we can therefore reject the null hypothesis, assuming that an improvement has been made in the yield, when in fact no improvement has occurred. The rejection region, although small, is still in the old distribution and such a yield is possible from it. This error is called an *α-error*. (2) The sample average can occur in the acceptance region and we can accept the null hypothesis that no improvement has been made, when in fact an improvement has occurred. As Figure 8–2 indicates, the acceptance region, although large, is overlapped by a portion of the new distribution, and the smaller the improvement effected, the more likely this is. This error is called a *ß-error*. If we study Figure 8–2, we see that there is a necessary trade-off in risk. If we decrease the chances of an *α-error*, we increase the chances of a *ß-error*.

Analysis of Variance

Hypothesis testing is a useful measurement device for a rather simple test in which only two means are involved. For measurements of more complex testing, the strategy of analysis of variance (ANOVA) is used. ANOVA is one of the strategies under the umbrella of design of experiments. The term is somewhat of a misnomer, because the method does not measure *variance*, which has a specific meaning. Analysis of variation would be a more accurate name. ANOVA strategy is this: a process is analyzed to determine the *factors*, or independent variables, that govern it. Discrete *levels*, that is, values of those factors, are judiciously selected for the test. The *response*, or dependent variables, are also identified. The *treatments* are the different test runs based on factor-level combination. ANOVA represents a break in traditional testing, which was based on varying only one factor at a time. Traditional strategy could not identify factor interaction, which is one of the major contributions of ANOVA.

The efficacy of ANOVA allows quite large experimental designs. For example, suppose that we were interested in analyzing the effects of certain conditions upon primary education. Let the conditions be our factors: (1) type of school; (2) type of student body; (3) type of school year. Then let the levels be (1) parochial and public; (2) gender integrated and gender segregated; (3) nine month and twelve month. Finally, let the response variables be scores in (1) reading, (2) composition, and (3) mathematics. ANOVA experiments would detect changes in the response variables with respect to any combination of factor and level, and would detect interactions also.

I choose this example partly to demonstrate the size of an experiment of which ANOVA can handle and partly out of mischief, believing that few people really want to know the answers to this experiment. A less controversial ANOVA experiment would be this: a brewer might wish to vary five ingredients in three different amounts to determine the effects upon flavor and yield.

Regression Analysis

This is one of the most widely used statistical procedures, along with analysis of variance. The idea is to describe the pattern found in random data by an equation relating the data (the response variable) to independent variables or factors. This idea can be seen in Figure 8–3, where response data are plotted with respect to a range of values of a factor of interest. In this case, a correlation is indicated by an increasing pattern, so by a method of least squares a straight line is generated. This line can be described exactly with an equation, and if the fit is good, the equation can be used for prediction. The benefits of regression analysis, in addition to allowing prediction, are that the measurement errors can be determined readily, and that the method is not limited either to single factors or to linear responses. Multiple regression allows measurement of response no matter what the number of factors. Of course, more than two factors puts the geometry beyond our view, but computers can determine high and low points, and other topological features in hyperspace.

Modeling with regression techniques incurs the same risk as any other kind of modeling, as we discussed in Chapter 5. That is, does the model used actually describe the relationship between the response and independent variables? Recall that Figure 5–6 showed the response curve of negative float with respect to a project schedule. The response has value only if the model is correct. So, too, Figure 8–3 has value only if our assumption is correct, that the data do indeed follow a linear relationship to the factor.

Regression analysis is so practical a tool that examples of its use overwhelm description. A few examples are test scores versus amount of homework; life expectancy versus smoking; rainfall versus season; lobster harvests versus an arbitrary time period; automobile sales versus income level and geographic region; and

FIGURE   8-3

Example of Simple Linear Regression

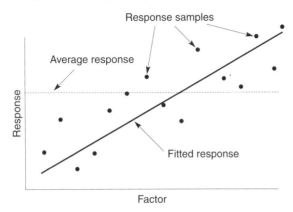

so on. Any relationship of two variables that has a random character is eligible for regression analysis. In the list just discussed, some of the relationships are linear; some are not. In the last case, there were two factors.

ON-LINE MEASUREMENT

Control Charting

We began this chapter by quoting Walter Shewart's comments about chance variation in measured product. The *chance causes* used by Shewart many years ago have come to be called *common causes* today. They are regarded as benign only because they are accepted as inherent in the system and must be lived with. Causes that result in variability outside the pattern have come to be called *special* or *assignable causes.* Assignable causes indicate unstable behavior of the system. They are not acceptable and resources are usually expended to eliminate them.

In order to identify and combat assignable causes, Shewart developed the method of measuring product variation that we call *control charting.* In Chapter 5, we saw that control charting not only measures variation, but determines whether the distribution is stable. The basis of the method is an assumption of a normal

F I G U R E   8–4

A Normal Distribution

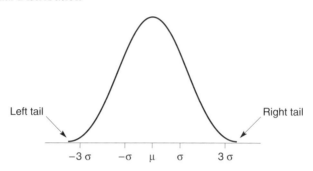

distribution of variation. However, the variation in industrial processes is not, in general, normally distributed. Shewart solved this problem by plotting the *averages* of samples rather than the values themselves, because the averages of distributions tend to be normal no matter what the parent distributions.

The normal distribution, or "bell curve," is so fundamental to statistics that it is worth the effort to understand a few of its values and symbols. The importance of the normal distribution is that its form and the area under it are well identified. As Figure 8–4 shows, it is symmetrical about its highest point, or center, which corresponds to the distribution mean. The first inflection point on either side of the center locates the $\pm 1\sigma$ values, and the area under the curve up to the $\pm 3\sigma$ point is 99.73 percent of the total area. This corresponds to a probability of 0.9973 that a sample will occur within the $\pm 3\sigma$ values of the distribution. The area beyond the $\pm 3\sigma$ points are called the tails. Samples that occur beyond the $\pm 3\sigma$ values are regarded as extremely unlikely (probability ≤ 0.0027) causes of system variance, and are therefore assumed with a probability of 0.9973 to represent special causes. A special cause may require a tough decision about intervening into the production process, but 0.9973 represents good odds. Management should like to have these odds in making all its decisions.

In Figure 5–3 of Chapter 5, we showed an example of a control chart of a variable quality characteristic. However, Shewart's

FIGURE   8–5

An Example of a p-Chart

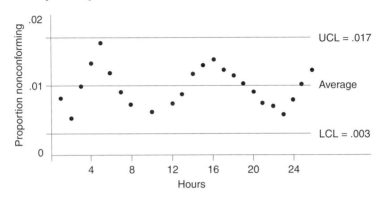

method is used with attributes also. In the context of control charting, an attribute is a quality characteristic that is measured as
either good or bad. Thus, an attribute inspection is a go/no-go
test, in which a product is inspected for attributes that are perceived to meet a criterion or not. A failure is considered a defect or
nonconformance. The advantage of attribute inspections is their
relative simplicity and lower cost. A typical attribute control chart
is shown in Figure 8–5. It differs in a number of respects from control charts for measured quality characteristics, most significantly
because the plotted variable is not an observed variable, but is a
ratio that must be computed from the observations, that is, it is the
ratio of the number of nonconformances found in a sample population over the total sampled population. In this figure, the greater
variation in the first eight hours might be due to, say, equipment
coming back on line after a weekend shutdown.

The recording of period *averages* of the quality characteristic,
rather than the individual values themselves, achieves normality
and enables estimates of process stability. However, a price is paid,
and that is the uncertainty of "liners," which are recordings on or
near the control limits. Since the recordings are averages of samples,
a liner might well contain a sample that is beyond the control
limits. Thus, the use of control charting requires a liner policy. For
example, a policy might be that the samples of each liner are to be

examined to see if any individual is beyond the control limit, and if so, to treat the event as though the average itself was over the line.

Control charting establishes *stability* of process, but it says nothing of *capability*.[1] Capability refers to the ability of a process to provide a product or service whose quality characteristics are consistently within specification. Notice that the limits on a control chart are control limits, that is, probability limits determined by the inherent randomness of the process itself. Specification limits do not appear on a control chart because there is nothing to compare them with. Only averages are plotted, not individual values. Capability can be determined from the data, though, and result in a parameter called a *capability index*. This index is the ratio of the specification limits to the control limits. An index of unity means that 99.73 percent of a company's product or service falls within specification limits. This is not considered very good because it means that there will still be 1,300 bad parts per million at either end of the limits. Bhote (1991) reports that 60 percent of American industry have not achieved an index of unity, whereas 1.33 was standard in Japan 15 years ago. Nevertheless, some American companies, notably Motorola, according to Gill (1990), are vigorously pursuing capability indices of 2 or better.

Finally, control charting doesn't control anything. It is not a control system in an engineering sense, but rather is a measurement system that provides data to enable control. Despite its several shortcomings, control charting is widely useful, finding a variety of manufacturing and service applications. A perusal of *Out of the Crisis* shows that Deming used it for all sorts of processes, from engineering changes to inspector performance variation to golf scores. I use it to monitor the gasoline consumption of my automobile. The mileage varies from about 25 to 35 miles per gallon. If a sample goes beyond control limits, I head for the garage for a tune-up or diagnostic.

It is important to realize that stability must be established *before* capability. We imagine, in business, that we want to make a good product, over and over. In fact, it must be done the other way around. First you make a product over and over, then you make it well. A process out of control can make good products randomly but not repeatedly. Stability must come first, and control charting provides a dependable measure of the stability of your processes.

Acceptance Sampling

When we receive parts from an outside source, we might consider whether to accept them or not depending upon their quality. Or we might be at the end of the production line and want to inspect our final product on the basis of its quality. This is called *acceptance inspection*, and it is done not by inspecting every item, but by sampling. The reason for this is the well-known fact that 100 percent inspection is not only expensive, but is not even fool-proof. Fatigue and human error contribute to inspection inaccuracies.

Acceptance sampling is governed by a sampling plan that is based upon a number of factors: the probability of defect of a single item; the distribution of defects; the lot size that the sample will be taken from; the sample size; and the acceptance number. The acceptance number is that number of nonconformances per sample that are acceptable. You might think that no defects should be acceptable, and sometimes that is the case. But in many circumstances the cost of zero defects is prohibitive. Therefore, the acceptance number can indeed be zero, but it might also be one, or several. Once these factors are determined, an operating characteristic curve, (called an OC curve) can be generated that will define the efficiency of the algorithm. Figure 8–6 shows a typical OC curve. Ideally, the curve should be a step function from one to zero, that is, the probability of acceptance should be unity for zero defects, and zero for any defects. Because of the nature of randomness and of inspections, an ideal response cannot happen. The best we can hope for is a very steep curve. In Figure 8–6, for example, there is a 50 percent chance of accepting a lot that is 2.5 percent defective. Is that good? Well, it depends upon how we want to define *consumer's and producer's risk.* The higher the probability of accepting a lot with significant failure rate, the higher the consumer's risk, because the consumer is going to buy from that lot. The lower the probability of accepting a lot with significant failure rate, the higher the probability of rejecting a "good" lot. The producer, then, increases his own risk. The probability of defect is inherent in the system, but risk can be adjusted by varying sample size and acceptance number. The dilemma is resolved by management decision, of course.

The idea of acceptance inspection is controversial among quality experts. As the saying goes, "you cannot inspect quality into a

FIGURE 8-6

A Characteristic Curve of Acceptance Sampling

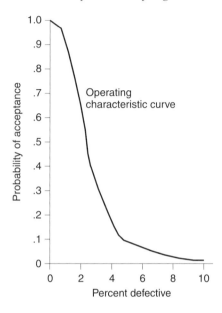

product." Therefore, why do acceptance sampling? Ryan (1989) suggests that you put your quality efforts into the product during production, make your suppliers do the same, and get rid of acceptance sampling as soon as possible. Yet, the technique remains popular among many manufacturers and service companies, and in fact, some have little choice. In ship repair, for example, many yards conduct acceptance testing on purchased valves, even though such valves may have a low failure rate. The reason is that the penalty for installing a bad valve in a ship can be severe, particularly if it is welded into place. Before the bad valve can be taken out, the work space and adjacent work spaces must be certified gas free, which will impact the ship work schedule. In sum, although theory may indicate that acceptance inspections are not a good idea, each manager must make his own decision on this based upon local conditions. Moreover, the decision may involve as many subjective as objective criteria.

IMPLEMENTATION

Statistical measurement has such broad application to industrial processes that it is difficult to imagine a business of any volume not using it. But Deming warns of the wrong use of statistical methods, in two areas in particular. The first is in wrong application and the second is in organization. There are hundreds of probability distribution models and the use of the wrong model may result in more harm than good. We get a lot of grace from the natural robustness of many of these distributions, but this robustness is a function of specific industrial features. Almost as bad as the wrong use of statistical methods is the wrong assignment within the organization. All too frequently, the quality control department has the purview of quality methods, including those statistical, to the exclusion of those actually accomplishing the processes.

Deming's solution to these problems includes an interesting idea, the creation of a staff position in statistical methodology. Many companies may object to such a specific position because of the tendency of humans to pedantry and empire building. However, let's focus on the objective: to achieve the correct and efficient use of statistical methods in all company processes. This goal can be attained by assigning statistical methodology as a corollary responsibility of the quality assurance department. Identified as a responsibility, it gets the necessary visibility. Widespread use is encouraged because QA departments usually have at least nominal entrée to every process in the company. Empire building is avoided because the actual quality methods and analysis will be conducted by those responsible for the processes.

Management at the highest level needs to support the measurement of its processes. When those responsible get to do the measuring, rather than "outsiders," they are encouraged to use the methods for improvement. The role of quality assurance in the matter is that of ensuring validity of application through joint meetings of process managers, supervisors, and workers, in which the details of theory and practice are worked out. It is important to include the workers because the charted process is often not the actual one. I know of production lines with ad hoc inspection points, a feature that has important statistical interpretation. The method must match the process.

NOTE

1. **Stability and Capability.** The normal distribution curve, the well-known "bell" curve, is symmetrical about its mean value, diminishing in long narrow tails. Of the area under this curve, 99.73 percent is contained within $\pm3\sigma$ limits. Thus, by placing control limits of an industrial process at the $\pm3\sigma$ limits of its variation, we are confident that 99.73 percent of the product will vary within these limits. Corollary to this reasoning is that if a measurement falls beyond the limits, the probability is .9973 that the measurement is due to a cause external to the process, that is, an assignable cause. Now consider the ratio of specification to control limits. If this ratio is less than unity, obviously the control limits are wider than the specs, and much of the product is out of tolerance. As the capability gets much larger than one, more and more of the normal tails of the variation fall within specs and the probability of producing nonconforming product becomes very small indeed. For example, an index of 2 means that only about four parts per million are beyond specs. Compare this to the 2,700 parts per million of an index of unity. Motorola's 6σ quality target is equivalent to a capability index of 2.

REFERENCES

Bhote, Keki R. *World Class Quality.* New York: AMACOM, a division of the American Management Association, 1991.

Deming, W. Edwards. *Out of the Crisis.* Cambridge, MA: The Center for Advanced Engineering Study, Massachusetts Institute of Technology, 1991.

Gill, Mark Stuart. "Stalking Six Sigma." *Business Month,* January 1990, pp. 42–46.

Ryan, Thomas P. *Statistical Methods for Quality Improvement.* New York: John Wiley & Sons, 1989.

Shewart, Walter A. *Economic Control of Quality of Manufactured Product.* Princeton, NJ: Van Nostrand, 1931.

9

⑥   CORRECTIVE PROCESSES

TRACKING QUALITY

All conservatism is based upon the idea that if you leave things
alone, you leave them as they are. But you do not. If you leave a
thing alone, you leave it to a torrent of change.

G. K. Chesterton, 1908

In Chapter 7, we described briefly the corrective action that might
be taken in the event of a defective product. Whether a nonconformance should require rework, scrap, or regrade is necessarily a
local decision. The goal of this chapter, as Chesterton's words suggest, is to maintain quality by correcting the process. This is
robustness. We assume that we've structured a stable and capable
system. Left alone, the process will change. In my experience,
change may begin slowly, but if left uncorrected it will increase
until some hard limit is met. Hard limits may be imposed to arrest
disaster, but they do not represent robustness. Correcting processes astray is itself a process, so our approach will be from that
point of view. As before, we will begin with some engineering concepts, then show how they are applied in business and industrial
processes.

    Correction is another word for control, or to put it more
accurately, correction is the objective of control. Real-time control

minimizes the buildup of errant behavior by providing timely correction. We will examine methods of automatic control: feedback, feedforward, gain, integration, and differentiation, showing when you use which, and what the mechanisms mean in business organizations. The goal will be to construct systems that respond correctly to change.

REACTING TO CHANGE

A system, its inputs, and its environment are all dynamic and interactive. Change in quality can come about through any or all of these media. The system can drift off its optimum settings, creating variation in state and output. The needs of the customer or supplier may change, representing a variation in input. The operational environment may be modified by some new rule or intervention. We shall call any of these changes to the status quo a *disturbance* and imply no negative connotation to the word. The disturbance may be deliberately applied, as an increase in lathe speed. It may be undesirable, as a machine breakdown. Whatever its nature, a disturbance forces a change in system state and we want the system to respond to the change in a desirable way. We will use the term *corrective action* to describe the things that we can do to ensure desirable response of the system to change.

When a disturbance acts upon a system, it forces the system from its existing state to some other. If the disturbance is very large it can drive even a stable system into instability, but even relatively minor disturbances require an appropriate response. In many cases the system will respond with some correction, although perhaps not quite as fast or as much as we want. This response may have a corrective nature even if no corrective process is built into the system, if only by dint of having humans in the loop. For example, a fire in the shop or office will bring about corrective action. In order to arrive at some idea of what appropriate corrective action is, let's look at some characteristic responses to various disturbances.

Figure 9–1 shows some examples of how an arbitrary system might react to various disturbances. The curves in bold type represent the disturbances, and the curves in light type are the system response. Unity gain is assumed for demonstrative purposes, so

FIGURE 9–1

System Responses to Various Disturbances

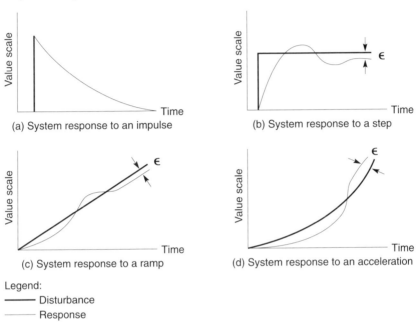

(a) System response to an impulse

(b) System response to a step

(c) System response to a ramp

(d) System response to an acceleration

Legend:
——— Disturbance
——— Response

that the response should equal the disturbance if the system were perfect. The disturbances are stylized here as well-known mathematical functions, but they approximate very closely a variety of real disturbances, deterministic and random.

Response characteristics are not always keyed to the disturbance alone. They may be keyed to the cause also. For example, assume an accelerating disturbance due to management decision, serial system failure, or changing economic environment. Corrective action may be designed to have faster or slower response appropriate either to the cause or to the disturbance. Similarly, a step disturbance may be due to machine failure, new corporate objectives, or electrical blackout. We may want to weigh the cause in designing the rapidity of response.

An impulse is a mathematical abstraction: a force of infinite magnitude and infinitesimal duration. But so many physically realizable events are impulsive that it is handy to define a real-life approximation. A commonly accepted definition is that an impulsive disturbance is one of arbitrary magnitude and whose duration is brief relative to the time constant of the system that it disturbs. An example might be that of a momentary power failure that knocks office equipment off line. If the process is stable, the system downtime will be short-lived, with operations soon back to normal. This type of response is shown in Figure 9–1(a). The system is stable, so that the response is transient and dies out, with the system returning to its predisturbance state.

A step disturbance is one that occurs almost instantaneously and does not die out, but maintains some constant amplitude. An example might be the addition of a second shift to the production line, calling for a higher output level as a new system start. In Figure 9–1(b), the system response to a step disturbance is somewhat sluggish, lagging behind the nominal value of the command. Sooner or later the response catches up, but then overshoots. Finally, the system settles out to a constant level—in this case somewhat less than that of the nominal. This is called *steady-state error*, denoted ϵ. Response time, overshoot, and steady-state error are all design features. We can improve them as we wish. Similar comments hold for the response to the ramp disturbance of Figure 9–1(c) and for the system reaction to the accelerating disturbance of Figure 9–1(d), except that in the latter, the error is arbitrarily shown greater than the nominal value.

A simple example will explain these ideas in business terms. New orders have come in and we want to increase the number of workers on the production line to meet the increased demand. We have a list of part-time workers who are usually available, and we call them in. The time that it takes to get to a new level of production is the response time. If the tasks are relatively simple, we can get to the new level almost as a step up, similar to the response of Figure 9–1(b). If the tasks require significant training, the new level of production will probably ramp up as shown in Figure 9–1(c). In this example there probably would not be any overshoot (too much production) unless we hired more people than we needed for our goal, or unless there was an initial high output of bad work due to lack of training. Finally, at some point we would achieve a

FIGURE   9–2

A Time-Shifted System Response

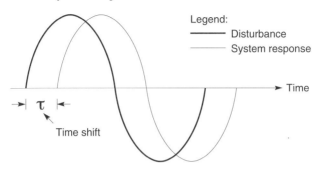

steady production, which may be slightly over or under our target (the steady-state error).

Figure 9–2 depicts a system that has responded to a cyclic disturbance exactly as expected in value scale, but the response is delayed by a time factor of τ units. Time delay[1] is yet another response characteristic that can be increased or decreased by design. Sometimes called a *transport lag* by engineers, time delay is both a commonly occurring phenomenon and a perspective. Industries in which material is piped from one location to another fall in this class. As a point of view, we might consider a production system as a time-shifted process in which each unit proceeds down the line τ units after its predecessor. This time-shifted delay can become an important quality variable when back orders exist.

In sum, change invokes response, and the response characteristics that a control system is to address are response delay, overshoot, settling time, steady-state error, and time delay. The first three are called *transient response* characteristics. Settling time is that period following the disturbance that it takes the system to arrive at a steady state. Desirable response characteristics can be established within a process either by changing the process itself or by inserting a controller into the larger system containing the process. We shall consider various configurations for automatic control as well as some of the controller processes themselves.

CONTROLLERS

It is one thing to anticipate change. It is another to prepare for it. Let's assume that we have a process whose dynamic response is not as good as we should wish. Anticipating a disturbance, we might consider it reasonable to go into the process and change its dynamics in some way. However, there are situations in which we might be reluctant to change an existing process. One example is an expensive and self-contained machine, under manufacturer's warranty. Another might be a finance department that works well internally, but whose interfaces need modification. The solution is to devise a *controller* to supplement the process. A controller is simply a mechanism that, together with the process, ensures a desired dynamic behavior. A controller is sometimes called a compensator or equalizer because it corrects for the shortcomings of the original process. A controller might be a hardware mechanism, a software program, or even a management decision system.

There are several basic ways in which compensation can be inserted into an existing process without changing the dynamics of the process itself. We begin by looking at things with a broader view so that the process whose response characteristics we want to change is encompassed in a larger system. Then we determine the system error, which will be the difference between what we want and what we have. Following this, we design and insert the controller.

In Figure 9–3(a), a controller process is inserted in series with the process to be controlled, and feeds forward. Alternatively, in Figure 9–3(b), the controller is in the feedback loop. The input to the controller in Figure 9–3(a) is called an *actuating error.*[2] It may not be the true system error because if the feedback mechanism has its own dynamics, then the feedback signal will not be exactly the system output. The controller then sees the difference between the reference and the feedback, not the difference between the reference (what we want) and the output (what we have).

It is possible to change either the *characteristic* response or the transient response of a system with a controller, so this is an important consideration. However, the configurations in Figure 9–3 have the same characteristic behavior, so the choice of where to locate the controller will depend upon the requirements and

F I G U R E 9–3

Several Configurations of Automatic Control Systems

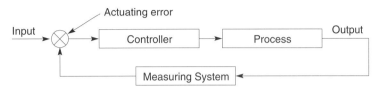

(a) System corrective action with controller in feedforward

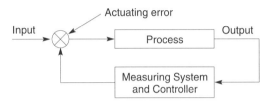

(b) System corrective action with controller in feedback

opportunities available at the site. There are permutations on the configurations shown in Figure 9–3; controllers can be put in parallel or in cascade to any subsystem in the feedforward or feedback line of a closed-loop control system.

When planning to insert some compensating or controlling action into a process, we need to keep three things in mind: (1) if we want to change the *system* containing a process rather than the *process* itself, we must be able to specify the prechange dynamic behavior of the system as well as the process whose response we want to improve; (2) the system perspective must be broad enough to encompass all those inputs, other processes, and environment that directly affect the process to be compensated; and (3) some controller configurations will change the transient response only, whereas others will change the characteristic behavior of the modified process or system.

An example will clarify these points. Suppose that we are a power company with a manual trouble-reporting process whose response time is too slow for customer satisfaction. We can install an automated system (changing the dynamics of the process itself), or we can assign more people from another office to the troubleshooting function during severe storm conditions when large numbers of power failures are expected (inserting a compensator into the system). Presumably, these persons have other things to do, so that the dynamic response of the larger system will be changed during the period of reconfiguration, perhaps adversely. We need to know the response characteristics of the *system* supporting the troubleshooting process both before and during reconfiguration, in order to properly evaluate whether the trade-offs have resulted in more gains than losses. Therefore, the general approach to determining an appropriate control configuration is to first determine how the existing process works and its configuration within its supporting system, then determine the goal, that is, the new response characteristics. At this point we can then begin thinking about controller type, configuration, and acceptable trade-offs.

We can add or subtract gain, or integrate or take the derivative of its action, in order to compensate for the dynamic properties of a process. The term *derivative* has several meanings in popular language, and so is ambiguous.[3] As engineers often do, we will use the term *rate* instead of derivative. Figure 9–4 shows combinations of these dynamics, presented in terms used by engineers. The letter K stands for the *gain* of the process, that is, the ratio of the power or value of the output over the input.[4] Since K can be greater or less than unity, gain acts as a proportional device. In Figure 9–4(a), the correction is *proportional* to the actuating error. If there is more than one element in the process, then each has its own gain, signified by K_i.

The letter S is known in engineering as the LaPlace operator.[5] It is a symbol of dynamism because it represents two kinds of change. S stands for rate of change, and its reciprocal, $1/S$, stands for integration.[6] Let's look at the latter case first. Integral control means that the *rate of change of the correction* is proportional to the actuating error. The operator is $1/S$. In Figure 9–4(b), we have proportional plus integral control, which combines the two types, assuring that both our correction *and* the rate of change of our correction are proportional to the actuating error. The relative weight of the two controls is established by their gains, K_1 and K_2. The meaning of proportional plus integral control, in everyday terms,

FIGURE 9–4

Various Controller Dynamics

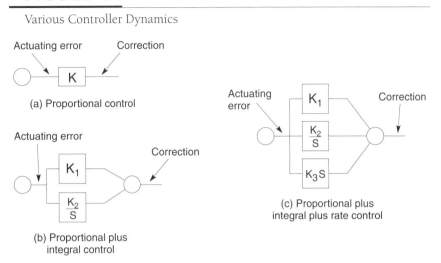

(a) Proportional control

(b) Proportional plus integral control

(c) Proportional plus integral plus rate control

is this: we want to correct for an error, and the larger it is, the more and the faster we want to correct for it. Delivery companies might use integral control to respond to increasing demand.[7]

Rate control means that the correction is proportional to the *rate of change of the actuating error.* The operator is S. Although rate control gives us a sensitivity to the change in error, it is never used by itself because it detects change only. It would not detect a steady error no matter how great.[8] In Figure 9–4(c), we have proportional plus integral plus rate control. Combining the three types, we ensure that both our correction *and* the rate of change of our correction are proportional to the actuating error *and* to the rate of change of the actuating error. Companies dealing in perishable goods and volatile markets might use rate control in order to anticipate customer movement.

We have discussed some of the theory of process correction in everyday terms. An understanding of these notions helps us to define and formalize corrective procedures in our business structures, once we have determined their equivalences in organizational terms. In the following section, we will devote most of our effort to this equivalence, concentrating the discussion in those industrial areas in which controllers, as such, are not well known.

IMPLEMENTATION

To reiterate, the purpose of corrective processes is not only to detect error, but to provide robustness. This is done by correcting or compensating for processes as they drift from a target state to some other. It does not matter whether the corrective processes are human or machine, management or labor, but they should be automatic, or nearly so. Processes that correct by disciplined procedures may be considered automatic if their response time is swift in relation to the process time constant. In other words, human intervention, properly organized, can provide robustness. This idea is important because in many cases the expense of automation exceeds the savings that it might provide. Should a company forgo hope of a robust process in such cases? No, any company can achieve robustness by systematic operation. You buy a machine by first ensuring that the specifications provide consistent, stable, and repeatable performance. Well, you can do the same thing with procedures if they are properly developed and rigorously and routinely performed. Let's keep this idea in mind when we discuss controlling actions.

There is a remarkable similarity to stable business organizations and closed-loop control systems, which is the germinal idea of this book. Sometimes the analogy is exact. This idea is not readily acceptable, though, because people object to the notion that *control* or *automaton* can or should apply to human beings. In fact, these words have negative connotations today. So let's approach the subject by asserting up front that we all have free will. We have a right to say no, and even have a right to be wrong. But in business we don't want to be wrong, and it is in our self-interest to work together in an integral way. This means doing things predictably, accurately, and consistently. It means controlled operations and systematic performance. In the diagram and discussions that follow, we will examine the similarity in control system and business structures, and the equivalence between control system parameters and organizational functions.

Figure 9–5 shows a control system with a major and minor controller. The general structure is similar to that shown in Figure 9–3(b), except that there are multiple control loops. The first dynamic block represents various initial processes that we might

An Example of Processes Configured for Corrective Action

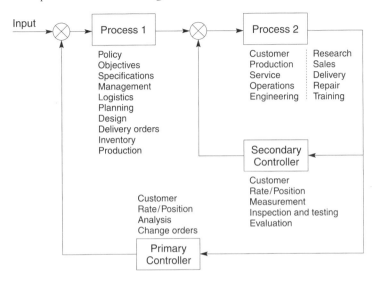

find in a business or military organization. The second block represents follow-on activities. The controllers are corrective processes and can be functions or operations, just as those shown in Figure 9–4. For example, the primary controller can be a rate sensor, value measurement (in this case, *position*), a customer input, or perhaps a change order. Whatever the function or operation, there is a dynamic to it. This means that it has a rate or integrating tendency, with gain. These properties hold whether or not we planned them, because that's what dynamism is. So let's examine what these things mean because it is better to design them than to allow them to develop on their own.

Gain Control: Authority

Simply put, the gain of a system is the ratio of its output amplitude to its input amplitude. This concept is easy to understand in electronics, for example, but its analogy in other domains is sometimes not fully appreciated. There must be an equivalent measure in a properly constructed business system. For example, consider *authority* as a control mechanism as described in Chapter 4. We know that authority is delegated to a person by a superior in order to achieve a task, also delegated. But the two delegations are often not in proportion because the superior may be reluctant to release authority for one reason or another. Thus, when we examine the control structure of a business organization we may see lines of responsibility in a closed form, all well and good. But the level of authority will be variable. Looking at this from the analogy of gain, we might say that if the authority is commensurate to the task, then the loop *gain* is unity. If the person has insufficient authority to do the job, then the gain is less than unity; authority more than required means the gain is greater than unity.

During an audit of a major shipyard, I was introduced to a project manager, responsible for the repair of an aircraft carrier. The cost of the project was about $180 million, which gives some idea of the magnitude of the job order. The project manager was unfamiliar with the work package or assignment of tasks, and had only a superficial understanding of work progress, although he seemed to know most of the players. These are symptoms of a man who had lost control of his project early on, and possibly never had it, because he had insufficient authority to accomplish the tasks. This authority was vested in the head of production, who also was line manager for the shops in the yard. Thus, men, material, and resources went to the job at the discretion of the production manager, not the project manager.

This is a familiar story to those who study matrix management. Weakly empowered project management is a common ailment in matrix organizations and is one of the major criticisms of it. However, the same weakness can be found in line organizations, which compensate for ineffective channels by redundancy, creating parallel channels. By drawing up the organizational structure in closed-loop form, and by considering the necessity for some equivalence to *gain*, we can more easily determine the effectiveness of the structure, or whether it is even possible. For each defined responsibility there should be one minor loop and a commensurate authority. For each minor loop there should be one unique responsibility.

Rate Control

There are many industries that deal with a cyclical environment. They are as disparate as fishing and clothing. When change is cyclical, forecasting is an appropriate and frequently used strategy. Other industries, however, must deal with aperiodic change that is difficult to predict, or in which errors in prediction are intolerable. For them it may be necessary to detect and correct immediately for a changing input or environment. We speak here of the sort of change that, although indeterminate and irregular, is nevertheless repetitive so that our processes must accommodate it. Rate control will do this. Since rate control implies that correction is proportional to the rate of change of the actuating error, the organizational structure should be designed to detect changes in either the process input, environment, or output. Let's identify some changes that frequently occur in systems operations, input, environment, and in the system or process itself. Once such changes are identified, we will discuss controller strategies, some of which are well known, others easily imagined, and still others requiring definition.

When a system and its environment are viewed broadly, a number of events can be identified whose rate of change may be sufficiently high that they must be tracked. The nature of the events depends upon the industry, but some examples are shown in Table 9–1. Some of the examples are the reciprocal of rate—they are expressed in time (period)—but the principle pertains. That is, tracking a period is equivalent to tracking a rate. Others are not rates at all, but can be converted to rates; for example, customer complaints can be converted to complaints per one thousand transactions.

Table 9–1 is meant to stimulate consideration of rate control. It is not definitive, nor are units of measurement provided. Each company must decide for itself whether it sustains events that are candidates for rate control, then must select the rates, determine metrics, create a closed-loop portrayal, locate the monitoring site, and establish the controller mechanism. Controlling mechanisms will also be specific to each circumstance, but presumably the essence will be immediate correction. Otherwise, why track rate? This may seem a simple idea, but I have seen service companies that can identify immediate customer needs immediately, yet take

T A B L E   9–1

Events that May Require Rate Control

Environmental	Input	Process
Technology changes	Specifications	Common causes
Regulations	Delivery orders	Assignable causes
Deregulations	Change orders	Technology upgrades
Competitive innovations	Material requirements	Personnel turnover
Inflation	Material costs	Personnel absences
Demand changes	Inventory	Maintenance periods
Supply changes	Documentation requirements	Failure events
Market size	Customer complaints	Repair times
Information	Database requirements	Equipment downtime
Transportation schedules	Sources	Discrepancy reports
Natural causes	Just-in-time activities	Training requirements

a week or more to respond. Just-in-time (JIT) inventory is an excellent example of the need to track, and meet, the rate of production. Introduced from Japan, JIT is being integrated into American methodology with increasing acceptance. However, Ansari and Modarress (1990) report that JIT requires quite a bit of unlearning of traditional American concepts on inventory. I visited a plant with large amounts of in-process inventory throughout the floor. Management's reason for tolerating the situation was that labor believed in-process inventory reflected job security.

There are many methods for tracking changes, among them forecasting, market research and analysis, database management systems, information technologies, and statistical process control (SPC). Although open loop, SPC provides both detection and tracking strategies. Methods have been developed to detect trends in industrial processes due to assignable cause. Cumulated sum charts and exponential smoothing forecasts are examples. However, these are detection and tracking, not control methods, so they must be augmented within the organization to effect correction. This does not mean that SPC is inefficient; on the contrary, in the general case, detection and correction will require two different mechanisms. The idea is to establish the closed-loop structure of the organization, identify the point of actuating error, then determine appropriate methods to detect and correct changes due to input, environment, or process output as measured at that point.

In principle, this strategy is valid for every industrial organization that can be structured in closed-loop form. Buch and Wetzel (1993) describe a similar strategy that they call *sociotechnical SPC*. They present an open system model of organizations that includes the environment as well as the subsystems themselves. The latter include managerial, political, cultural, social, and technical subsystems. Still others prefer the term *statistical quality control*, or SQC, to refer to the application of SPC methods to the larger organization. SQC strategies apply to any kind of process with uncertain parameters, including rates, that can be measured.

Integral Control

All the things that were said about the need for rate control apply to integral control. The difference between them is technical, not philosophical. Integral control means that the *rate of change of the correction* is proportional to the actuating error. Whether we use rate or integral control depends partly on circumstances and partly on subjective judgment. Some customers are viewed as more valuable than others, some inputs more critical, so that we may choose a rate of correction to reflect the status of the input. As we said earlier, the best controllers are a combination of the different control strategies. The most comprehensive is, of course, proportional plus rate plus integral, which provides that both correction *and* the rate of change of correction are proportional to the actuating error *and* to the rate of change of the actuating error.

Implementation of controllers is not free, so that a great deal of thought must go into the appropriate correcting strategy. It is absolutely essential that the controller mechanism be able to detect, track, and correct systematically and in a timely way. If the mechanism is procedural, then it is all the more important that management support the controller with documentation, training, policy, and custom.

In sum, the use of engineering analogies and structures in the design of process control provides for a disciplined, analytical result. The technique is routine and straightforward if the processes are physical. Some thought is required if the process is man-machine or organizational. The reward, however, is a system that is robust to any foreseeable disturbance.

NOTES

1. **Time Delay.** The phenomenon of a variable value reproduced exactly but delayed in time occurs so often that it has picked up many names: time delay, transport delay, transport lag, or even just lag. However, *lag* has other specific meanings to engineers and statisticians, so that we use the term *time delay*. Basically, if a physical system involves movement of energy over distances such that time is not negligible, then time delay occurs. A few examples are process industries, transportation, and economic systems.

2. **Actuating Error.** A controller is a device for closing the loop in a control system by providing corrections to the system when what it does diverges from what it is supposed to do. Clearly, it needs an input that expresses what this difference is. This difference is called an *actuating error*. The actuating error may be the difference between the system output and its input, in which case it is called, reasonably enough, *system error*. But in general this will not be the case, because in measuring the output, we will introduce dynamics that will be fed back to the comparator. Thus, the comparator will see not the input and the output, but rather the input and a feedback signal. This difference is the actuating error that will drive the controller to make a correction. A very simple yet accurate example is this: you are the manager of a process and want to compare the difference between what your process is supposed to do and what it does, but you don't have time to make the comparison yourself so you have someone else do it, and report to you. His report is the basis of your corrective action.

3. **Derivative.** At the time of this writing, *derivative investments* have been much in the news, and since few people understand what they are, including myself, this term seems to cause more ambiguity than ever on just what *derivative* means. We won't have a problem with it in this book, though, because we shall use the term strictly within its mathematical meaning. The derivative is one of two of the main ideas of the calculus. It refers to the rate of change of some dependent variable with respect to the rate of change of an independent variable. More specifically, it examines this rate of change in the limit, as the

change in the independent variable gets infinitesimally small. The independent variable may be *time*. For this reason, engineers often refer to a derivative as a *rate*, although mathematicians hate this practice and scorn engineers for doing so. However, engineers are guilty of many mathematical sins, too numerous to be listed here, among them that we will call a derivative a rate even if the independent variable is not time. For example, customer complaints per one thousand transactions is a rate. Mea culpa, mea culpa, mea maxima culpa. Since the change in rates is examined in the limit, that is, infinitesimally small, it follows that the variables must be continuous. If the variables are discrete, one refers to their rate as *differences*. But again, that is often too inconvenient for engineers. In this book, we won't worry too much about whether the rates of change are continuous or discrete, but will assume that the sampling rate for measurement will be appropriate to the rate of change being measured. A rule of thumb is that you should measure a changing variable ten times faster than its own frequency.

4. **Gain.** The *gain* of a process is, roughly speaking, the ratio of the amplitude of its output to that of its input. I say "roughly speaking" because *gain* is usually defined in terms of a specific reference input, say a sine wave or exponential signal, or an input power. In this respect, it is analogous to the *decibel* (db). We often hear of noise at 110 db, but, in fact, this has no meaning unless the input noise level is established. So it is with gain. The input reference must be established. The gain ratio is a constant (a single number) for linear systems, which makes it a nice quality index. However, according to Šiljak (1969), nonlinear systems have only incremental gain, which means that it is not constant over the operational range. Thus, for nonlinear systems the concept has little value.

5. **LaPlace Operator.** Symbols have long been used to indicate when certain mathematical operations are to be performed. Some of the most easily recognized are: +, ÷, and √. Less popular symbols, yet commonly used in the mathematical disciplines, are ∫ for integration, and **D** for differentiation. Because these symbols dictate an operation to be performed, they are often called operators. The LaPlace operator is symbolized by **S,** and operates only in the LaPlace domain. This subject bears some explanation. The study of dynamic systems became feasible with the development of the calculus by Isaac Newton and Gottfried Leibniz early in the 18th century. Nevertheless, analysis was difficult for all but very simple systems because of the complexity of calculation. Pierre Simon De LaPlace (1749–1827) developed a method for transforming differential equations to algebraic equations in order

to simplify solution. It is easier to multiply than to differentiate; it is easier to divide than to integrate. The LaPlace transformation is used often in the study of dynamic systems because of this ability to simplify the calculations of time-driven mathematical models. It is common to use the **S** symbol wherever convenient, with the understanding that it operates only in the transformed domain.

6. **Integration.** Integration means one thing in mathematics, another in organizations. In mathematics, integration is the other of the two main ideas of the calculus. It is the estimation of a quantity by summation of many infinitesimal pieces of it. For example, integration finds the area of a figure by summing up the very small areas of a very large number of narrow rectangles superimposed on the figure. This "summing up" strategy is used only for demonstration today, but is the origin of the symbol ∫ used for integration. In this sense, then, the similarity of mathematical and general understanding of integration is apparent. It has to do with summing things together in a systematic way. *Summing up* is the universal definition of integration and the one used in this book.

7. **Integral Control.** Integral control means that the *rate of change of the correction* is proportional to the actuating error. In the inventory analogy, we don't care how fast the inventory diminishes, but we will reorder greater amounts the lower the level. Integral control is thus a form of rate control, and not an integration as understood in the general sense. It is called "integral" because engineers insist that if a rate exists on the input to a lag, then the output must be its integral.

8. **Rate Control.** A system is a process. In this book, the terms are used interchangeably. A system is defined by its input, output, and state. In the absence of control, the system responds as well as it can to a given input, but this response may be unsatisfactory and even unstable—thus the rationale of control of process dynamics. Rate control means that if a system output diverges from its desired value, a correction is generated that is proportional to the *rate of change of the actuating error.* We also want proportional control, because if the error is constant, our rate detector won't sense it, no matter how large. Inventory presents a ready example. We want to measure not only the rate of use of our inventory, but also its level, for we may use the level as a reorder trigger.

REFERENCES

Ansari, A., and B. Modarress. *Just-In-Time Purchasing*. New York: Free Press, 1990.

Buch, Kim; Charlotte Wetzel; and David Wetzel. "The Evolution of SPC in Manufacturing." *Journal for Quality and Participation,* October/November 1993, pp. 34–37.

Chesterton, G. K. *Orthodoxy*. New York: Lane Publishing Company, 1909.

Šiljak, Dragoslav D. *Nonlinear Systems*. New York: John Wiley & Sons, 1969.

10

⑥ DYNAMIC IMPROVEMENT

LET KNOWLEDGE GROW

Good reasons must, of force, give place to better.

William Shakespeare

In 1972 I attempted the task of tracking down a medal that my uncle had been awarded by the French government for valor in World War I. After many months of frustration with delays and noncommittance with embassies and bureaus on both sides of the ocean, I began to realize that the usual strategies would go nowhere. Spying a nondescript document in my uncle's dossier, I saw that it was written in 1922 from a small office entitled *Association des Anciens Combattants de Verdun,* and appeared to be a citation. The citation gave the telephone number and the address of the bureau, and was signed by the secretary, a Monsieur Panau. After writing the bureau to inquire about a reissue of the medal, I received in short order a new medal with an accompanying letter. The bureau still had the same address, the same telephone number, and the same secretary. The signature was a little shaky, but it was clearly Monsieur Panau, 50 years later. Talk about stability! Customer satisfaction, too.

Few organizations enjoy such a stable environment. We live in dynamic times, and no matter how good the product or service, in the words of Shakespeare, we must do better. Of course, this sounds good and everyone says it. To get beyond the cliché, though, to get better consistently, we need to achieve dynamic improvement, the ability to do better automatically and systematically. We can do this with robust mechanisms.

Corrective processes are a necessary but not sufficient complement of robust systems. They are necessary because they supply the mechanisms for convergence to target value. They are not sufficient because the target value of original design is a constant, whereas dynamic improvement implies a moving target. However, we are not seers and cannot rely on prophesy to detect changing forces to meet or lead demand. The essence of dynamic improvement is knowledge. The more we know about an environment or an input range, the better our predictive and deductive abilities. The timely use of knowledge for continual improvement of process is at the heart of an improvement program. This knowledge must be appropriately implemented and integrated into the corporate process structure. We are therefore interested in the acquisition and application of knowledge, the range and reach of process structure, and the dynamics of integration. The latter subject is central to systems philosophy and so will be postponed to Chapter 11, where it will be discussed at length.

THE EXPERT SYSTEM

Improvement begins with being aware that there is a better way to do something, or that the customer is interested in a new product or a new feature in an old product, or that the environment is changing. The basis of improvement, therefore, is knowledge. But if we want to use knowledge efficiently, we need to distinguish its many facets because they are exploited in different ways. There are three words that are tossed around often these days as though they were interchangeable: data, information, and knowledge. We should always be suspicious when three words mean the same thing because it indicates fuzziness. Fuzzy expressions lead to (or reflect) fuzzy thinking and misunderstanding, so let's say what we mean. We'll start with *data,* the most primitive of the three. The dictionary definition is as good as any: data are facts and figures from which conclusions can be drawn.

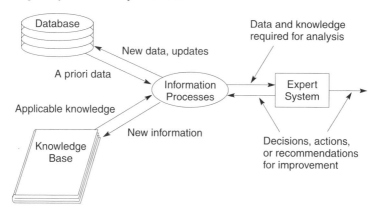

FIGURE 10-1

An Expert System for Improvement

Distinguishing between knowledge and information is a little tougher because in general usage they mean the same thing. They both imply *knowing*, but it seems to me that knowledge implies more than this. There is a sense of *reason* and of *wisdom* associated with the notion of knowledge. The meaning of information, on the other hand, is somewhat pre-empted, at least in the technical world, because it has been rigorously and narrowly defined by Shannon (1949) in his development of information theory.[1] It refers to data that literally *informs* us, data from which we can draw conclusions with a certain probability. There is no information in the statement: "life is followed by death." The conclusion is certain—we knew it before the datum was received. There is a great deal of information in the statement: "There will be a storm tomorrow."

The three forms—data, information, and knowledge—are often expressed in rather fashionable terms: database management, information technology, and expert systems. We can unite all this in a cohesive way by thinking of them as a larger system, as shown in Figure 10–1. This arrangement helps to formalize the process of using information to effect an improvement mechanism. The figure may be rather confusing because there is a block called "expert system," and yet the whole figure is called the same thing. This confusion can be cleared away after we've defined a few terms.

An expert system is a computer program that uses the knowledge of experts to solve problems, make decisions, and offer recommendations.[2] The range of reflection may be quite narrow. For example, the *tactical data* and *command and decision* programs used by the U.S. Navy 20 years ago were certainly expert systems. In this application, the objective was to rapidly evaluate a threat scenario within a noisy environment, then select the optimum engagement doctrine. Expert systems provide more than speed. They can offer multicriteria decision capability in complex environments. And they have the virtue of reliability of all software programs— once right they are always right.[3] This ability in speed, complexity, and consistency makes expert systems a core asset for handling knowledge and achieving automatic and systematic improvement.

Yet, we humble humans are experts, too. We think extremely slowly, and can process only one variable at a time in our mental closed loop. Somehow, though, we have managed to stumble through evolution, and on the way, have even invented computers. We have imagination, the ability to distinguish nuance, to see into the future a little bit, to deduct, and to induce. Bearing this in mind, look at Figure 10–1 again. In this figure, as in all figures in this book, think of the blocks as *functions,* not as machines. In every case, a function can be achieved by either a human or a machine, with corresponding trade-offs. Therefore, companies that lack the breadth or volume of production to justify the cost of expert systems can still implement the functions. Let's redefine an expert system then: an expert system is a process that uses the knowledge of experts to solve problems, make decisions, and offer recommendations.

The structure of the expert system shown in Figure 10–1 is a closed-loop feedback system. Each element is united with every other in a dual transmit-receive arrangement. An improvement system fits into a larger closed-loop system as a subsystem, as shown early on in Chapter 1, Figure 1–3. As we discussed in Chapter 6, Figure 1–3 represents an arbitrary aggregate level. It could be a view of a corporation, a company, or a process activity. The improvement mechanism will be appropriate to the level.

The knowledge base is that reservoir of knowledge, understanding, and methodologies that reflect what we know about the process, its environment, its input range, and possibilities of change. Knowledge methodologies are forecasting techniques, brainstorming sessions, libraries, market and technology analyses, and information processes that we use to keep our knowledge current and vision wide. As much of this base as possible should be resident in the expert system program, but not all of it can be. The reason is that the resident base is fixed and cannot adapt to improvement targets beyond its limits. But, as Deming says, improvement must go on forever because the environment will change forever. Therefore, the knowledge base is dynamic and its contribution to the expert system should be ongoing. That is why I refer to the larger assembly of Figure 10–1 as the "expert system"; the computer program, no matter how sophisticated, is a subsystem of the total process. Information is exchanged between the program and the knowledge base because the program should increase our knowledge in a synergistic process.

The database is that reservoir of facts and figures that describe the process, its environment, its input range, and probabilities of change. The database is also dynamic and is more accurately a database management system (DBMS). As much of this base as possible should be resident in the expert system program, but again, not all of it can be. Similar comments to those of the knowledge base pertain here. And again, the DBMS is updated by the expert system in a synergistic relationship.

The expert system program, supported by databases, knowledge bases, and information processes, forms a dynamic larger system that we will agree is our *expert system*. It is a decision maker. It does analyses, evaluations, and comparisons. Expert systems analyze multiple objectives against constraints or aspirations, and rank alternatives. Based on these analyses it can make decisions or recommendations, and take actions, depending upon its empowerment. The empowerment is governed by humans. For example, Navy tactical data systems operate under the concept of command by negation. In automatic mode they can evaluate a threat scenario and engage a target, subject to human intervention. Unless a human says nay, the target will be destroyed. In manual mode they evaluate the scenario and make a recommendation.

The expert system recommendations include information that can be used to educate the market. Improvement cannot reasonably be separated from customer expectations. The airline industry is a good example of never-ending customer dissatisfaction because to a great extent, profitable operations conflict with customer comfort. The industry spends a lot of money on touting its services, which increases customer expectations. Then the customer arrives at the airport, and it's all downhill from there. The troubles of the airline industry might be unsolvable, but for most industries customer satisfaction is possible provided expectations are educated. Not brainwashed. Educated. Real improvement comes about in a symbiotic relationship between the customer and our product or service, based upon the feasible. The expert system can help to establish what we might call the *feasible region* of product or service.

We repeat the point that expert systems do, by definition, what human beings do. That is why the expert system can be tailored to the needs of the company, both in capability and in automation. Even relatively small companies can implement an expert capability. A personal computer of modest capacity is inescapable, if only for database management and for analytical algorithms. An expert system of arbitrary size, and with some of the operations being exercised by humans, must still provide all of the expert system functions in order to have a meaningful improvement program. In addition, certain operational features are required. As Hertz (1988) lists them, they will be real time user-computer interaction, well-defined rules for inferences and interpretation, provision of diagnostics and recommendations, an accurate portrayal of key processes, and an ability to integrate information.

REACH AND RANGE

The expert system provides us with the closed-loop mechanism for improvement of process at any level in the company. But what is it that we actually vary for improvement? And what are the improvement indices? We'll approach this matter through the notion of reach and range. For our purposes, *reach* describes the indices of performance improvement, which in coarse terms are quality and productivity. The metrics of quality and productivity are up to the individual company, but some suggestions are shown in Table 10–1. *Range* refers to the processes that we want to improve. We might argue whether we want to improve product or

T A B L E   10–1

The Reach and Range of Improvement

Reach: Quality Index	Reach: Productivity Index	Range: Candidate Process
Customer satisfaction	Labor	Asset utilization
Capability	Material	Capacity
Stability	Inventory	Capital investment
Variation	Overhead	Market response
Average value	Transportation	Objectives
Acceptance criteria	Marketing	Research
Rate criteria	Sales	Resources
Time criteria	Training	Sources
Cost of quality	Testing	Technology

process; again, this is the purview of the company, but in this book we are focused on process. The reason is that our entire approach is *system* oriented, and I believe that improvement of process yields improvement of product, and is the only consistent way in which product can be improved. Table 10–1 shows candidate processes. As with the indices of reach, the processes are at a rather high level of aggregation. Each can be broken down into lower levels of process, and necessarily will be, once a program of improvement is decided upon by the appropriate levels of management. This is necessary because at the action level things must be named, and we have a better chance for success if we precisely define exactly what will be improved and how we will measure it.

The columns of Table 10–1 appear similar—lists of factors. But they are meant to be used differently. The *reach* factors are indices. Pick one (or more) and assign a scale to it. The *range* factors are the processes to be improved. Let's review some examples. Suppose that in our business, we are primarily concerned about customer satisfaction. We determine a method and metric such as polling and number of complaints per one thousand customers, then establish a scale for rating. The scale will be either a raw score, for example, ten complaints per thousand, or a normalized scale, say a percentage of an acceptable raw score. We then make our improvement adjustment to the process of concern and evaluate the process according to this scale. In this way, we measure the improvement in terms of a preferred quality index.

Contrary to a popular slogan, quality is not free, although it is necessary if you want to stay in business. Usually there are trade-offs that a company must make in order to avoid diminishing returns in going for quality. Often, the trade-off is measured in terms of productivity. As a result, we may decide to track productivity simultaneously with quality for every program of improvement. Productivity is typically measured by dividing "output" by the number of labor hours needed to produce the output. This is a rather coarse measurement, good enough for government indices perhaps, but not fine enough to use for measuring improvement of a specific process. The column of productivity lists a number of factors, and as with the quality column, we pick one. We may pick labor but choose to measure indirect or overhead costs charged against the labor of a process. Whatever our index, we develop a method and metric, then measure the effect of an improvement program in terms of both quality and productivity. It is likely that they are mutually conflicting in the critical region of our improvement range, so that an optimum point must be found in the measurement.

These ideas are shown in Figure 10–2, where all of the processes are listed on the *process* axis. Actually, we may wish to plot the quality and productivity indices with a single process, assuming that we can determine a scale for it, so that we can determine the optimum point of quality and productivity values for a particular process improvement. Nevertheless, a plot of several related processes, as shown in the figure, may also be informative, if there are interactive quality and productivity effects among several processes when one of them is changed.

The candidate processes are coarsely defined, too. We may have a specific asset whose utilization needs to be improved, or we may be considering a specific capital investment or increase in capacity. Sometimes, of course, we can do these calculations in our head. Some years ago I visited a small Ma and Pa winery in Solano County, California. This was about the time when American interest in wines was beginning to explode, and corporate giants such as Heublein and Seagrams were moving into the business. That

F I G U R E   10–2

A Surface Response in the Reach–Range Space of Improvement

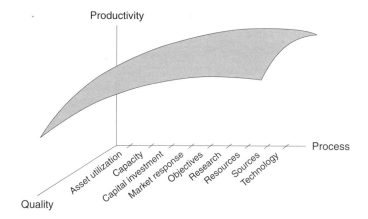

day, some visiting New Yorkers were attempting to convince the owner that, his wines being good, he should "go big time." The old timer just shook his head negatively. His wines *were* good. From the point of view of quality, he had attained his reach and range. Further expansion would require significant capital layout without any assurance that he could increase either parameter. He chose not to take the gamble, and it is a choice that every entrepreneur must consider when bounding his improvement capability. Can I increase sales? Can I offer as good or better product? How much will it cost me, and what is my risk?

No business is too small to neglect the reach and range of its processes, although sometimes the optimum values are easy to see. My wife's family had a friend in St. Emilion, France, who made his living with *one* hectare of vineyards. A hectare is about two and a half acres. His volume was small and his variety was singular. The processes included manual plowing. He did not sell T-shirts and he did not hold festivals. He sold wine. In general, we don't hold to modest ideas in America. In contrast to the wine maker in Solano County and the vigneron of St. Emilion, most American wine makers go for large volume and great variety. On the other hand, many of them complain of marginal profits. Clearly, bigger is not necessarily better. Reach and range analysis provides a means of relating quality and productivity to our processes in a measurable way. We first establish if improvement is even possible, then how much and in which direction.

No business is too large to neglect the reach and range of its processes, although the process aggregation level must be effective. In some cases, subprocess improvement is intuitive. For example, sourcing strategies might include supplier performance evaluations. As an independent consultant, I am surprised at how infrequently this is done. Nevertheless, supplier evaluation is a good idea. We might review the ability of a supplier to keep to delivery schedules, and we might maintain statistical evaluations of his products, with say, acceptance testing. In the latter case, the process is evaluated directly to a quality index, with productivity improvement implied. Generally, there will be some productivity evaluation, if only the keeping of pricing records in order to detect lowballing.

Lowballing is a particularly malevolent practice among government contractors and subcontractors because the government often seeks low bidders, and its contracts require the prime contractor to seek out low bid sources. A few years ago, an east coast shipyard bid and won a ship repair contract that was *50 percent* below the government's own expectation, then commenced to run the final bill to about *150 percent* above their bid. At least part of the overrun was due to the prime contractor facing high supplier costs himself. The only way that the "prime" can avoid the low bidder is to provide to the government significant data to show that the subcontractor is either nonresponsive, undependable, or a poor performer. Of course, the government is not subject to market forces and will never go broke. Neither, then, will its favorite contractors. Nevertheless, most contractors, including government contractors, want to provide good service or product, and for them, reach and range analysis is essential.

The list of processes includes objectives because of the rapidly changing external environment. Factors that were once considered more or less constant now change seemingly annually: public education, the natural environment, health care requirements, technology, and the explosion of new products from the global competition. The American automobile industry is a ready example of loss of market share due to changing demands in safety, pollution,

F I G U R E   10–3

Improvement System and Environment

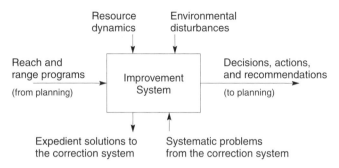

technology, fuel consumption, and style. Their production process was flexible—Detroit changed styles superficially every year. The industry suffered from an inability to sense fundamental external dynamics or to change objectives, or both. In any case, it was a *process* failure.

No process is too high in the hierarchy to be above consideration for improvement in goals, policies, or strategies. No process is too low. ISO 9000 auditors often speak of their purview as processes that affect the quality of the product, but it is hard to imagine an efficient enterprise supporting processes that do not affect the product in some way, because reach and range are pervasive. Secondly, the evaluation of process in terms of quality and productivity should be quantitative where possible. Qualitative and intuitive evaluations cannot find the best improvement levels and may even be wrong.

IMPLEMENTATION

Figure 10–3 shows the improvement system extracted from Chapter 1 for ease of reference. We design an improvement process and insert it in our overall system so that it can provide both short-term and long-term improvements. The long-term improvements derive from the reach and range programs of the planning function. This does not mean that they are not initiated from the on-line process, but whatever the genesis, the improved design has gone through a formal reach and range analysis. Short-term improvements, on the other hand, are those that derive from within the affected process by local experts to satisfy an immediate need or benefit. They go directly to the corrective function, and may become long-term improvements if they meet the formal criteria.

The improvement process enjoys a certain consensus. Fontaine and Robinette (1994) identify a sequence of steps: recognizing the opportunities, selecting one on a priority basis, analyzing the root causes of the existing problem or deficiency, determining a solution, testing it under controlled conditions, implementing the solution, then tracking the effect for improvement. Langley et al. (1994) describe a similar algorithm, spending more time up front, brainstorming the objective, and delineating expectations from the existing process. They then propose implementing the improvement process by means of a Deming cycle similar to that of Figure 3–3. The iteration is somewhat different in this case: Plan-Do-Study-Act, where the study refers to gaining knowledge through analysis. Rozum (1994) presents yet again a similar routine, but presents it in a concise matrix of evaluation. One column represents the objectives as determined by meetings with the customer. Another identifies the areas (processes) to be improved in order to meet the objectives. A third column lists the metrics that have been determined for measurement of progress. Finally, a series of ten columns is used for evaluating results on a quantitative scale.

These alternatives for implementing improvement are essentially reach and range programs; similar in form, they differ on detail and focus. The basis of the reach and range method is that improvement begins with the customer. This includes the *internal customer*, the process expert. Most companies have suggestion programs in recognition of the expertise of their employees, but generally they are run randomly. As we discussed in Chapter 2, employee participation must be systematic and focused on process improvement. This provides the genesis. Expert systems and reach and range strategy provide the mechanism.

We have seen that corrective and improvement processes are quite similar, the former looking back to see what doesn't track the existing objectives, the latter looking forward to new and presumably better objectives. Robustness is the result. But there remains one important capability: the integration of the many processes that make up the total system. In the next chapter we will discuss how to put it all together.

NOTES

1. **Information.** Specifically, Shannon has defined information as the freedom of choice one has in selecting from a number of messages. This is a very useful definition in the design of communication systems because it focuses on the totality of messages that a system must handle, be the messages words, music, art, electrical pulses, or whatever. It is an unsatisfactory definition to the general public because it is at first blush not in agreement with the common use of the word. It implies nothing of meaning, for example. But further consideration of Shannon's theory provides a connection. There is a property of nature inherent in the Shannon definition of information that is called *entropy*. It describes the randomness of the message pool, so that, to Shannon, entropy and information are the same thing, and unity less relative entropy equals redundancy. Thus the connection. The less redundancy in a message, the higher its relative entropy, or information.

   Entropy. Entropy is a characteristic found in certain natural events that was first identified in natural philosophy, and is particularly associated with the second law of thermodynamics. You can't understand entropy without first considering this original introduction. Thermodynamics is the study of the relationship between heat and work, which are forms of energy. Thermodynamic processes exchange heat and work. The first law states that whatever the exchange, total energy is conserved. However, it is known that although all of a given amount of work can be converted to heat, not all of a given amount of heat can be converted to work. The second law recognizes this fact in so many words, but no way of expressing the second law quantitatively could be found until the concept of *entropy* was developed. Experiment showed that heat had two measurable components: energy that could be directed to work, and disorder. The disorder is called entropy. The second law states that a natural process will always take place in the direction of greater disorder, or entropy. Therefore, systems tend to states of greater disorder—thus, the loss of efficiency in the conversion of heat to work. Disorder is random and uncontrollable without putting added energy into the system from an external source.

   Shannon's genius was that by defining information as an entropic quantity, he could show a natural order to communication. Some of the resultant experiments are startling. For example, assume that we have 26 letters and a space, therefore 27 symbols. Then let us begin choosing randomly from this pool. Entropy is high for the first choice because each symbol is equally probable of being selected. But suppose that the first letter chosen is "T." Then, in English, there is less choice in the selection of a second letter because of the rules of the language. We cannot select "J" at all, and "H" is more likely than "Y." Thus, the freedom of choice is narrowed, as some symbols are less probable of being selected than others. Entropy is lowered by selecting in groups of two symbols. The freedom of choice continues to decline when selections are made in groups of three, four, and five symbols. At the same time, we find that the groups of symbols increasingly resemble the English language even though syntax and meaning are completely absent. As entropy decreases, redundancy increases and the structure of English can be identified.

2. **Expert System.** Waterman (1986) defines an expert system in this way: "a computer program using expert knowledge to attain high levels of performance in a narrow problem area." Although valid at the time it was made, time is leaving this definition behind. Expert systems are applications deriving from the dynamic field of artificial intelligence. As we learn how humans think, particularly experts, we derive ways to implement this process in computers. Much progress has been made in recent years so that Waterman's constraint about narrow problem areas is somewhat ambiguous. First, it is now possible to get a wide variety of databases in a single computer so that many different kinds of problems can be resolved expertly. Thus, expert systems are no longer very narrow in scope. Secondly, module integration, algorithm processing, and pattern recognition are becoming more efficient, so that it is feasible to process larger numbers of synapses and nodes within a given problem. Thus, expert systems are no longer very narrow in depth. Finally, as I say in Chapter 10, only partly facetiously, humans are experts too, and I dislike restricting the notion of expert systems to costly embedded computer complexes.

3. **Reliability.** Traditionally, reliability is an index of operating durability of hardware. The metric is usually time, so that the longer in time that a unit can operate without failure, the higher its reliability index. This unit is so informative that it has been adapted to software also, but not without controversy. Once correct, a software program *never* fails. However, it takes a long time to get a complex program correct, and as program bugs are found, the time from last bug to latest bug is considered operational time, and an index of reliability. Technically,

though, the bug was always there, inadvertently put in by the programmer. The program did not really fail with time in the same sense that hardware fails with time. As Fox (1982) asserts, correct software cannot fail, and what you are really measuring in a time measure of software failure is not the system error distribution, but the customer use distribution. Some experts, for example, Neufelder (1993), avoid the controversy by defining reliability for software differently than for hardware. This presents an additional problem, though, because her definition is not in units of time, and resembles a *quality* index more than a *reliability* index. All this sounds like scientific nit picking, but really it is not. In measuring things, it is extremely important that you identify what it is that you are measuring.

REFERENCES

Deming, W. Edwards. *Out of the Crisis.* Cambridge, MA: The Center for Advanced Engineering Study, Massachusetts Institute of Technology, 1991.

Fontaine, Daniel J., and Diane B. Robinette. "FCC Makes Dramatic Quality Improvements." *Quality Progress,* November 1994, pp. 87–91.

Fox, Joseph M. *Software and Its Development.* Englewood Cliffs, NJ: Prentice Hall, 1982.

Hertz, David Bendel. *The Expert Executive.* New York: John Wiley & Sons, 1988.

Langley, Gerald J.; Kevin M. Nolan; and Thomas W. Nolan. "The Foundation of Improvement." *Quality Progress,* June 1994, pp. 81–86.

Neufelder, Ann Marie. *Ensuring Software Reliability.* New York: Marcel Dekker, Inc., 1993.

Rozum, James. "A Way to Improve Customer Satisfaction." *Quality Progress,* October 1994, pp. 67–71.

Shakespeare, William. *Julius Caesar.* Act IV, Scene 3. The Great Books. Chicago: Encyclopaedia Britannica, Inc., 1952.

Shannon, Claude E., and Warren Weaver. *The Mathematical Theory of Communication.* Champaign, IL: University of Illinois Press, 1949.

Waterman, Donald A. *A Guide to Expert Systems.* Reading, MA: Addison Wesley, 1986.

11

⑥ PUTTING IT
ALL TOGETHER

THE INTEGRANDS

No one can question the importance of executive leadership to focus a total organization on improvement. Nevertheless, improvement, however it is conceived, planned, or initiated, almost invariably comes down to the cooperative actions of teams of people.

D. C. Kinlaw, 1992

We've discussed at length the process of putting together a robust organization. We begin by doing nothing. We first kick back and just think—think about what we want to do and where we want to go. We assign a mission for ourselves that embraces our goals and destiny, then determine policies that will get us there. We establish goals and ways to measure those goals so that, having put our policies into action, we shall know when we arrive. Then, and only then, do we design and assemble the processes of action. No matter what their function, they are all designed in the same format, a closed-loop feedback system, because closed loops accommodate corrective and improvement mechanisms. Having done all this, we are far from finished even with the initial phase of our effort. We need to get all the processes to work together, to integrate them into a cohesive whole. Integration is fundamental to achieving a corrective and self-improving process.

In mathematics, the functions to be integrated are called *inte-grands*. In organizations, the functions, or integrands, are all the processes that compose the company. And yet a company may put together an integrated organization chart, but somehow integration does not obtain or is random. Part of the reason is that the processes must be integrable, and we will discuss this technical detail in a moment. But the other reason may be that the will is not there. As shown in Figure 11–1, effective integration requires an explicit effort to integrate people and planning. Planning has a special status because it is uniquely the management purview and because it initiates everything else. People have a special status because they run all the processes. For integration to succeed there must be cooperation, which by its very nature requires the will of everyone, not just that of the CEO. Integration requires cooperative people, interactive planning, and integrable processes.

Kinlaw (1992) asserts that to achieve real integration, we have to get beyond that found on organizational charts and into people-to-people integration. If this is true, then many industries are in a world of trouble because of the adversarial relationship established between management and labor. Some companies claim that people are their stock-in-trade. Let's assume that where so many clichés abound, there may be truth, that people are indeed fundamental to achieving robustness. We will explore the evidence of this and discuss various strategies for improving the process by improving the use of people.

EMPOWERMENT

> He believed in a worker who saw his interests as identical to those of the company. He wanted above all, a worker who used his own mind and his own experience to improve his own job, the product, the process, and the quality.
>
> *Peter Drucker, speaking of Tom Watson, Sr., IBM's founder, 1986*

Empowerment is the rage these days. Open a trade journal or business magazine and you will read about the importance of empowerment. CEOs proclaim, to a chorus of hallelujahs from quality gurus, that we must empower the worker. Even the politicians are using the term, which attests to its popularity. But what does

F I G U R E   11–1

The Integrands of Robust Systems

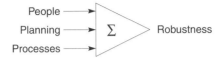

empowerment really mean, and how successful has its implementation been? Does management really walk the talk?

The basis of empowerment is the recognition that people are usually competent in what they do. They have a valuable bottom-up view. They are experienced and have a strong vested interest in doing what they think is necessary. Senior management is usually not as competent as those they supervise in carrying out the tasks of the processes in which they have purview. We want to take advantage of this reality by designing systems that will attract competent persons and encourage them to do their best. This is what Tom Watson, Sr., believed in, and he was irrefutably successful. Empowerment is meant to provide this encouragement and to bring out this capability by providing the employee with the tools and decision-making authority needed to achieve the task, thereby instilling pride and self-confidence.

In an earlier age, the workforce was overwhelmingly craft oriented and the condition of empowerment was the rule. In a small business, the entrepreneur employed a few craftsmen and, recognizing their individual importance to his production, by and large left them to do what must be done. There was no managerial class. The entrepreneur ran the business and the artisans crafted the product.

The arrival of mass production changed all this. Relying heavily on machines operated by less skilled workers, entrepreneurs increased production to unimaginably high volumes, realizing large profits at low cost of labor. As time went by, a managerial class grew to administer the whole thing. On the other hand, workers saw themselves in a role of diminishing importance, which in many industries eventually reached the level of automaton. They retaliated by joining industrial unions in large numbers. The more they were stripped of any semblance of pride of craftsmanship, the more compensation they demanded. Several years ago there was a television documentary of a wedding ring factory in Brooklyn, New York, that I found terribly sad. The fabrication of a wedding ring was done in a series of steps on an assembly line. Only the last worker got to see what the final product looked like, and that person could scarcely claim pride of authorship. Ever since then, when I have wanted a ring, I have bought one from a street artisan.

The transition of our economy from craftsmanship to industry saw the creation of two alienations. The first was the alienation between management and labor. The root cause is generally blamed on a disagreement of compensation, but I believe that there is another—the human tendency to amass authority. Management at all levels gathers authority, and at the supervisory level the only authority to amass is that over the task itself. This has led to the second alienation: the worker from his job. No one wants to be an automaton. If forced into this role, the worker tends to slovenliness and absenteeism, and quality suffers. Benign neglect or malicious compliance becomes the rule.

Today, probably due to the intensity of global competition, there seems to be an increasing rapprochement between management and labor, an apparent willingness to find common interests. For example, fewer employees join labor unions than in earlier generations. On the other hand, management talks a more enlightened talk, expressing a willingness to *drive out fear*, as Deming puts it. We hear words about *empowerment* of the worker. But is this apparent disarmament of antagonisms taking place on both sides? Do workers now enjoy the confidence of their leaders, or conversely? Simmerman (1994) provides some interesting statistics:

> Study 1: *89% of office workers believe that it is very important that management provide the tools and resources needed to get the job done, but only 51% are satisfied that they have this provision.*
> Study 2: *88% of executives believe that employee participation is important to productivity, but only 30% of their companies do a good job involving employees in decisions that affect them. Only 38% of employees report that their companies do a good job of seeking their opinions and suggestions. When opinions are sought, only 29% of employees say their company acts on the suggestions.*
> Study 3: *Of 250,000 workers at 60 companies, only 48% believe their bosses listen to them; only 60% believe their bosses keep them informed.*

Study 4: Of 1,237 workers in a Gallup Poll, 36% said they were not involved in quality improvement. Only 15% were empowered to make decisions in their jobs. Only 29% said they were satisfied with their company's efforts at quality improvement.

These numbers indicate that the transition from resistance to cooperation falls short of expectations. Perhaps the whole subject is more complex than we imagine. In a section called "Is Hierarchy All that Bad?" Tomasko (1993) provides evidence that empowerment of employees is an idea that must be used with care. As hierarchy is reduced, anxiety increases. The role of middle management in coordination and integration of work flows can be delegated, but they also have a role of psychological protection against anxiety and fear of the unknown. Managers are paid to think about an ambiguous tomorrow. Workers with specific tasks to do today often display irrational behavior when empowered to also worry about the future.

Improvement means change, but how that change is introduced into the company has a great deal to do with its acceptance among employees. Lowenthal (1994) says that while management might recognize the need for change, they often implement it wrong, believing that employee behavior is changed by altering a company's formal structure and system. In fact, Lowenthal asserts, individual behavior is shaped by the roles that people play in the organization and that the most effective way to change behavior is to put people into new roles.

Perhaps. Assigning people to new roles can create more problems than solutions if it is done as a management mandate. It is human to find comfort in a familiar niche. We become experts in doing the same thing for a sustained period. A new assignment sends the employee out without the shield of recognized expertise. The solution is training, but real, professional level training follows new assignments surprisingly seldom. On-the-job training (OJT) is cheaper. It also instills less confidence and strains the management-worker relationship even further.

The achievement of a close relationship of workers and management depends to a certain extent upon the processes themselves and the sort of workforce that is required to carry them out. Hersey and Blanchard (1982) have developed a matrix that delineates the various kinds of relationships, breaking them into four categories. The first is the *Tell* mode of management, the 19th century style. Management views the workforce as parents view children, and tell people what they must do and how they must do it. As Gibson (1990) notes, there may be some justification for this style of management when the labor force is immigrant, cannot speak English, and performs rote chores. In a mature industry of skilled workers, the Tell mode is unacceptable because the management–worker relationship is purely authoritarian.

The next level of management style, according to the Hersey–Blanchard theory, is the *Sell* mode, in which management tries to persuade the workers that following management ideas in performing the tasks is in their own self-interest. There is still no question, though, that the how and why of the tasks are dictated by management. Whether the persuasion is effective or not, the management–worker relationship is still authoritarian and not in keeping with modern ideas of quality and improvement.

The *Participate* mode is yet a higher level of management style. Here, the workforce is considered skilled and knowledgeable about production processes, and their opinion is solicited by management. According to Gibson, white-collar workers have long enjoyed participation as defined at this level, and many blue-collar workers are equally ready to participate in the decisions relevant to their skills. The participate level of the management–worker relationship is the minimum level acceptable to a total quality management program, and is fairly widely used in American industry today. Yet, the data of the Simmerman studies indicate that it is still not sufficient for self-improvement processes.

The *Delegate* mode is the highest level of the management–worker relationship identified by Hersey–Blanchard. Workers are "self-actualized" and capable of organizing themselves to their tasks. As Gibson puts it, the management role is more of consultant than leader. The Delegate level seems to be the most efficient for self-improving processes, and corresponds to what we today call empowerment. But, as Tomasko explains, certain traditional management roles cannot be delegated. The farther down the chain of command, the less likely that the worker will have the breadth of view to make decisions integrable with the business environment. Many people see this shortcoming in themselves, which increases their uneasiness about empowerment. Kinni (1994)

F I G U R E   11–2

The Hersey–Blanchard Modes in Terms of Employee Empowerment

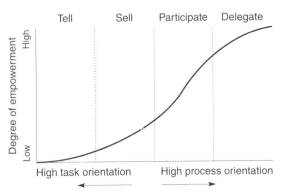

estimates that about 5 percent of the workforce simply cannot deal with it.

Figure 11–2 relates the Hersey–Blanchard modes of management–worker relationships to the degree of employee empowerment. The crux of empowerment is that it is highly *process* oriented, demanding that the employee have, in addition to an expertise in his task, an understanding of the process. This means that he must have a systems or panoramic view: inputs, outputs, objectives, and environment. Many employees seek this out from an inherent curiosity. I should guess, for example, that the overwhelming majority of systems engineers are self-trained, driven to go beyond their position descriptions in order to satisfy an internal need to "see the big picture." They seek this out on their own because the tendency of management is to constrain labor to specialization. Why spend money to train someone to a level of understanding that he doesn't need in order to accomplish a specific task? The problem with this narrow view is that it is self-defeating. It is a *policy*, which means that large groups of employees, perhaps everyone but management, are subject to it. But management are usually not experts in the technical arena of their purview, so that a policy of specialization means that there will be little systems level understanding of what the company does.[1]

If empowerment is to work, if management is to walk the talk, there must be a willingness on its part to provide system level training to employees so that they can attain the necessary level of understanding to contribute to robustness. With a top-down view of their particular processes, the employees will have a sense of adequacy and be encouraged to make decisions and recommendations about those processes. It is true that the top-down view is completely different from bottom-up experience, but the two do not conflict. On the contrary, the two views provide positive feedback and are mutually maturing.

THE CORPORATE TEAM

The importance of individuals, *as individuals,* to grand efforts has long been debated. The argument can be demonstrated by the following example. Irrespective of the efforts of thousands of men in battle and hundreds in the political arena, one man was crucial. The United States would have foundered if not for George Washington. Furthermore, the Confederate States might have succeeded if they had a George Washington. Whether or not this viewpoint is correct, no one designs a system about a specific person except perhaps a professional football team. We want each individual to do his best, but there are two parts to doing so. The individual part is this, that we do our best when so encouraged. Empowerment is one of the strategies that can contribute to this. But most companies are assemblies of unified processes, so that there is a group part to doing our best also. Since we can't do our best in a joint effort unless there is cooperation, the Tom Watson idea requires a corporate team, an *all-for-one, one-for-all* unity. This unity must be active between and among management and labor.

There are two generally recognized inertias in opposition to a unity of effort. The first is a resistance or inability to adapt to change, and the second is an opposition to empowerment, that is, delegation of authority. I submit that there is a third, often called the *rice bowl* mentality, or "you keep out of my business and I'll keep out of yours." This human tendency is widespread, although its roots are not clear. Do people build a moat around their function from a desire for security or in order to build an empire? I knew a man who was the government point of contact for a new weapons system during its development phase, about two years. Despite the need to know, none of his peers ever received a word of information from him. The system was installed on the first ships, and teams were sent for acceptance testing having little notion of how the system worked. We had to learn on site. On paper, of course, we were well prepared because organizationally, opportunities for cooperation were unbounded. In fact, no cooperation existed. We could not penetrate this man's walls without whistle-blowing to higher-level management.

Cooperation requires the support of an integrated organizational structure, which we will discuss in the next section. Beyond this, the best way to encourage cooperation and coordination is through the creation of teams. This must be done with care. There are many examples of successful use of teams, one of which, called *stall building*, kills two birds with one stone. In the stall building concept of production, an entire product, say an automobile, is assembled by a team at a single site, the *stall*. The company gets the efficiency of a focus of skills, and the workers get to see their efforts reach fruition from beginning of assembly to final product, so that they gain pride of authorship. In addition, to relieve the boredom of repetitive work, the team can rotate the tasks within the process among themselves.

Tomasko warns, however, that creating teams is often a way to get around dysfunctional organization. He advises differentiating between *teams* and *teamwork*. If we follow that advice, we might suggest creating a team within a process, and teamwork between processes, using mechanisms such as meetings and temporary cross-functional teams. The team-within-a-process concept would be similar to the stall building idea. Teamwork is achieved by a cross-functional effort between teams of distinct processes whose objectives require convergence. In this case, team integration through meetings and joint productive efforts brings about (1) a symbiotic understanding of processes other than our own; (2) acquaintance with other teams and acceptance of them as internal customers; and (3) a larger view of the enterprise and our place in it.

Building a team is not easy, and the reason has little to do with a "we versus they" barrier, which itself does not occur naturally. It's just that individuality is so greatly emphasized in America that if young people don't play sports, they may never be introduced to the idea of teamwork before adulthood. Gibson often complained that although engineers *always* work in teams, engineering students almost never do; they study alone at the university and compete with each other for grades rather than cooperate. Of course, the Armed Forces have a rather traumatic way of establishing a team concept quickly. We can discard the Armed Forces *style* of installing teamwork as unworkable for civilians, but we ought to look *carefully* at its components.

The way to establish teamwork is to recognize, as the Armed Forces do, that the team is a microcosm of the company. It needs a mission, policies, and objectives, as well as control of its processes. It needs a leader and a horizon. If the team is within a process, the leader should be the process supervisor, but if the team is cross-functional, the leader should be regarded as a peer of the other process supervisors, acting as coordinator, point of contact, or chairman, for purposes of efficiency. We don't want to construct an *ex officio* hierarchy within the organization. We cannot have duplicate bosses, *anywhere.* This circumstance occurs surprisingly frequently in organizations, and sows frustration and resentment among the workers, who find themselves trying to satisfy two masters with incoherent or conflicting requirements.

The purpose of the horizon is to pace the effort. A project can create an intense esprit of cooperation for a brief period of time. Building a team esprit for a short period is fairly easy to do and is incredibly exciting. You focus on the objective and the team esprit happens. I have had the grand pleasure of being a part of teams putting out such intense, round-the-clock effort that successful completion of the project was exultant. Such team efforts create an affection and pride among the members much like a battle or football game, but cannot be sustained over a long horizon. On the other hand, the pace of a long-term program should be such to allow the players to grow respect for one another. Rather than a passionate drive for the objective, this mutual respect and understanding are cultivated as one of the objectives of the team effort.

INTEGRATION

We said that effective integration calls for a triad of effort, cooperation being just one of the elements. Planning for integration is a second. The Executive Officer of every fighting ship in the United

States Navy conducts a planning board for training meeting weekly. Every department head is in attendance. In some cases cross-functional or jointly functional training is to be planned. In other cases the individual department training programs are independent, but resources are not. For example, the engineering department cannot schedule casualty drills at the same time that the weapons department is conducting operability tests. Here it is not the training, but time, that must be integrated.

The analogy holds true for industry. On a typical day in any manufacturing plant, equipments are scheduled for maintenance, inventory accumulates, VIP visitors arrive, customers are demanding delivery, and engineering wants to conduct studies on the assembly line. These evolutions tend to fall into an area that we might call "the cracks" in the sense that they are extraprocedural relative to one process or another. Even intraprocedural evolutions can fall between the cracks on shared resources. The job order of one ship overhaul called for simultaneous landing of two guns aboard ship. Parallel landing requires two installation teams and two cranes or the work will be serial, not parallel, no matter what the schedule says. In this case there was planning but not integrated planning. Some key person, perhaps the yard superintendent or production manager, was missing on the day that the evolution was planned.

Integration through planning involves more than timely, shared distribution of resources. Persons representing diverse groups with common interests are required to participate in a joint planning effort. Common interest always exists between sequential processes, but as we noted in the shipyard example, even parallel processes may have common interests in needed resources. There are also nested interests, that is, the requirements of subprocesses within processes. Processes at the same aggregate level require horizontally integrated planning and nested interests require vertically integrated planning. It should not be presumed that the representative of a given process attending a cross-functional meeting has the depth of expertise appropriate to his function. However, it is his responsibility to ensure that the depth is there. Integrated planning requires that all parts of an organization at the same level and below should be planned for simultaneously and interdependently.

Additionally, every plan is based upon assumptions. The plan pertains to distinct processes each with its own function and resource requirements so that the assumptions must be considered *and tracked* with each process and subprocess in mind. By definition, assumptions are hypotheses that we accept as true; unfortunately, once assumed, we forget that they are not certainly true, but are only probably true. The probability of each assumption may not be constant across the system, but may vary from process to process. A simple example is this: a company, responding to demand, may decide to go to three shifts daily, assuming that all the processes can absorb the strain or that all maintenance can be postponed. Another more complicated example concerns a company that makes multiple products sharing certain subprocesses, and assumes that its overall process variance is due to the varying defect rates of each type of product, and not to the process itself. We regularly make assumptions about sales, costs, inventory, and other variables, implicitly including constant probability to all the processes subject to the assumption.

Subprocesses labor under the assumptions about the overall process, so that there is a nested effect. Consideration of subprocesses rather than processes requires only a change of perspective. For example, consider a vacation agency that is putting together a package for a weekend of dining, theater, hotels, and airfare. They arrange for discounts with the various activities under the assumption that the demand for the entire package is uniform. Then the product is put on the market and they find that although the demand for the package is about that estimated, there is an even greater demand on the part of local residents for the dining and theater activities. Thus, the assumption concerning the package was invalid for some of the activities. The agency may lose money on its commitment to hotels and airlines, or lose opportunity on its commitment to the restaurants and theaters. If general assumptions are made relative to a system, there is a need for tracking the assumptions relative to the processes of the system in order to determine variable interaction and to change the plans accordingly.

These ideas are shown graphically in Figure 11–3. Common interests are shown as boundary regions between serial and parallel processes in order to emphasize the importance of integration. Integration deals especially with those activities "between

F I G U R E 11–3

Boundaries of Common Interests and Assumptions between
Processes and Subprocesses

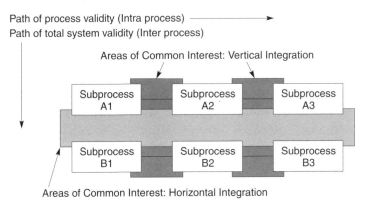

the cracks." On the other hand, the assumptions pertain to the processes and subprocesses themselves. In sum, we have achieved interactive planning when common interests are planned for, and assumptions are considered and tracked across and through the processes of the system.

The third leg of the integration triad is the *integrability* of the processes. This property is independent of people and planning; incompatible systems cannot be integrated no matter what the esprit or plans put into them. The systems of information technology provide clear examples. Purchasers of computer systems quickly find that a dearth of universal standards means that differences between vendors' hardware and software prevent linkage. In many of these cases nonintegration is planned and deliberate, as some vendors wish to isolate their market. In other cases incompatibility is inadvertent or occurs because of the high rate of change in the industry.

Integrability requires congruence of the processes and an integrating mechanism. MacKenzie's (1986) insight and experience on these issues are worth examining here. The integrating mechanism must be a common predecessor integrating process, not more than two levels higher than the processes to be integrated, and preferably at the same level. This is an important constraint because it implies that command functions that reach down through lower-level processes by jumping intermediate functions are maladaptive. They provide redundant, remote, and/or inexpert integrating supervision. The term *supervision* as used here does not necessarily imply human supervision, but is used as a function, much as *controller* has been used in this book. Integration does not just happen. There must be an integrating dynamic.

Congruence means that the processes to be integrated agree in goals, logic, architecture, environment, and resources. Systems engineers usually ensure that process logic and architecture are congruent when the system is designed. The remaining components of congruence are often overlooked, buried in organizational structure, or postponed to operations and then forgotten about. Congruence with respect to organizational structure can be tested for correspondence of the organization chart to the way the task processes have been assembled, to the communications network between activities, and to the allocation of resources among the activities. In a completely effective system, there would be no inadvertent redundancy. Each process would be serially dependent upon its predecessor process only.

Congruence with respect to resources refers to the allocation of resources in accordance with organizational logic. This seems to be a straightforward idea, and yet most companies suffer from a conflict of resource allocations at one time or another. When allocation problems occur, they are invariably due to competitive requirements, and so must be integrated, too. The problem becomes quite complex because of the diverse nature of resources. We usually have little problem imagining the allocations of resources that are identifiable to a process, such as locations, personnel, hardware, technology, and information. Our problems compound with those things that must be shared by widely diverse processes, especially time and money.

For example, money is a measure of the cost effectiveness of a process, but most processes neither stand alone nor have a directly measurable market value. Tracing the economic consequences of every process is too complex and in the final analysis, arbitrary. Most task processes work in conjunction with others, so that congruence of processes in terms of capital resources must be evaluated at the system level. Generally, the closer the process to the customer, the more value management attaches to it, not because it *is* more valuable, but because it is more easily measured. Yet, the *design* of a product must certainly be as valuable as its *sale.* Perhaps more, because if it is poorly designed, repeat customers will be few. In hard times, designers are laid off in greater proportion than production workers and salesmen, and this may make sense if a business is assuming a fallback position. But the steady-state allocation of capital resources should be based upon the direct relation of a process to quality.

Time is the most difficult of resources to allocate if, as in the general case, the events of a schedule are uncertain. For example, consider a long-term project such as the building or repair of a ship or of an airport, which may require hundreds of work items to complete. In general, this is a stochastic process. For large projects, one cannot predict with certainty the performance period of a single work item, much less the period of the project. The usual way to incorporate uncertainty in a schedule is to factor in an appropriate distribution, then compute most likely, least likely, and optimistic estimates. The results are usually called early and late start dates and early and late finish dates. The problem with this, according to Toelle (1990), is that the estimates are based upon mean values instead of variances. Toelle advocates defining critical activities based upon variance, then concentrating management attention on these activities throughout the project period. Lapin (1981), recognizing the inadequacy of scheduling on mean values, recommends simulation studies to determine the schedule. If time is to be allocated to activities, then the stochastic nature of those activities must be addressed. Let's define Toelle's critical activities as the U.S. Navy defines *controlling work items:* those activities either on the critical path, or by virtue of scope, complexity, material, or other considerations, have potential to impact the scheduled completion date. Then time should be allocated with mean *and* variance considered, and with close control by management of the controlling activities.

We have discussed the allocation of money and time, but as MacKenzie points out, when the need for any kind of resource for one process overlaps that of another, an interdependency is created. Interdependencies do more than complicate our conduct of processes; they confound our projections as well. The reason is that projections are often based upon probability models constructed from independent events, joint probabilities being frequently unknown. A basic goal of management should be to strive for congruence of resource use to avoid interdependency.

The whole purpose of integration is to achieve a synergistic sum from the outputs of two or more processes. If we have taken the correct approach, the synergistic result was the first objective; component processes are the means to getting there. Figure 11–3 indicates that this integration takes place both horizontally and vertically in the organizational structure. We can define these ideas in the following terms. Horizontal integration is used to achieve control of a system output as it is sequenced through a series of processes. Vertical integration is used to achieve control of a system output as it is sequenced through parallel processes.

IMPLEMENTATION

Employee Rights and Responsibilities

Putting it all together begins with getting everyone together, and that begins with empowerment. Kinni says that the foundation of empowerment lies in the obvious assumption that none of us alone is as smart as all of us together. I'm not sure that this is obvious at all, unfortunately, although I wish it were. For example, a belief in the superiority of collective wisdom is the foundation of democracy, but we all recognize the many oligarchies that remain at war with this principle. We find these oligarchies within corporations too. This book is written for those who can accept the idea that empowerment offers more than it costs, and the only question is how best to implement it.

There are a number of strategies for getting labor and management on the same page. A moment ago we referred to a political analogy in talking about collective wisdom. The comparison is apt in most cases because whether politics or business, we are talking about social relationships. As responsibilities must be associated with rights, so also responsibilities are associated with power. When we implement empowerment we need to tie new

T A B L E   11–1

Rights and Responsibilities of Empowerment

Right	Responsibility
Share in the corporate vision	Support the vision
Participate in goals	Strive for the goals
Derive empowerment from job	Fulfill job requirements
Training continuously	Maximize use of training
Participate in forums	Contribute to discussion
Share in financial information	Perform job cost consciously

responsibilities to them. Kinni expands on this idea with a worker's bill of rights. These ideas are repeated in Table 11–1, with the addition of one more right—a financial one.

When we study these rights of empowerment, it becomes clear that empowerment means a sharing of all facets of corporate management, from corporate mission through production to delivery. Even financial information should be shared, according to Christison (1994). This serves two purposes. The first is that sharing financial information reveals to the worker the constraints under which management must operate, and so provides answers to why certain decisions are made. The second is that it adds to the maturity of the worker's viewpoint and adds to his understanding of the financial implications of the way he goes about his job.

I remember years ago, as a telephone cable splicer, seeing great amounts of solder being wasted. We knew from observation that the Japanese cable splicer did not waste solder, but we just assumed that the difference was a cultural thing. If we had been made aware that waste added to the cost of production we would have been much more careful. Of course, the awareness must be made appropriately. Haranguing the employee about cost is the wrong way. That may be the way we teach our children, but an employee is not a child. The correct way to improve the cost of doing business within the context of empowerment is to let the employee see the same financial picture as does management, and let him come to realize that it is in his own self-interest to be cost conscious. As with all the rights and responsibilities of empowerment, there is a training requirement for the financial aspect. The training should be oriented from the top down, presenting an overview of the factors helpful to understanding, but then focusing in more detail on the cost and profit factors of the job itself.

Training Programs

We claim that employee empowerment is the key to personnel integration and that training is the keystone of empowerment. It provides competence and self-assurance that an employee needs in order to contribute to robustness. This is certainly true of management, and most companies do not spare the horses in providing training for its leaders. Training of all employees is equally important *to the company.* However, the data show that American companies are not very good at this. Lamprecht (1993) reports that whereas Japanese firms train their employees more than 300 hours during the first six months of employment, U.S. workers receive less than 50 hours. Assistance from the average state training programs just goes to companies with over 200 employees. Small firms, which account for 35 percent of American jobs, often have no training budget, whereas large firms often hire personnel already trained. Brecka and Rubach (1995) report that only about 0.5 percent of American companies account for 90 percent of the $30 billion spent on training annually. This sounds as though big companies train and little ones don't, but the reality is even more bleak. Many national companies have appallingly small training budgets. These statistics can be turned around by implementing a reasonable, cost-effective training program. Most companies don't need a training department with huge staff, but with a little thought can take advantage of available facilities and training aids. Let's begin with the requirements.

A training program should be in proportion to the job. A few jobs are quite simple. Many are very complex. None should be a dead end. Each employee should have a training program tailored to his needs, and it should include the following elements:

1. Identification of training needs.
2. Provision of the training.

3. Assurance that only qualified people perform a given task.
4. Maintenance of training records.

Identification of Training Needs

This is the area that is often underestimated. It is the wrong place to scrimp. Training requirements include now and future, theory and hands on, product and process, customer requirements, and quality improvement. The employee should be encouraged to broaden his perspective, to take courses that improve inductive and deductive reasoning. One might ask, why should a welder, for example, need to use reasoning beyond the quality of the weld? I can talk all day about the challenges that workers face beyond the strict application of their jobs, but a few examples will suffice. I have seen rocket launchers installed on ships in such a way as to shoot down the ship's fan antennas. Why? Because the drawings were in error. I have seen radio frequency waveguides installed in such a way as to create huge power losses. Why? Because the ship structure differed from the drawings. In each case, the error was obvious. All we need to do to avoid this sort of thing is to have employees with a bigger picture of where their task fits into the scheme of things, then encourage them to think about it.

The first element of the training process should be the big picture view—where the employee fits into the organization and why, and where his task fits into the organization and why. This puts things into perspective and prepares the employee to consider his task as a process with inputs and outputs, suppliers and customers, and himself as a member of a team. The training should then focus in on his particular process. This should include both the technical requirements and the system perspective. His supplier is the person *upstream* in the larger process; his customer is the person downstream. A knowledge of input and output requirements makes the employee an effective part of the whole, and a perspective of the *state* of his process or task makes the employee better able to evaluate dynamic quality.

When technical competence in process operation is achieved, follow-up training should focus on quality. Quality training should be both abstract and specific, that is, the principles of quality should be taught, and then the employee should be shown how they apply to the job. This process encourages reasoning. Quality training should include statistical process control, diagnostic tools, and continuous improvement strategies. All this is worked out in a team effort of worker, associates, and supervisor. Application of training can be encouraged by pay raises and other recognition forms associated with education and utilization goals.

Provision of the Training

There is a wide variety of effective training media: company classroom, company laboratory, OJT, and community college. The latter is often overlooked, but in most states the community college system is oriented to support local industry with both theoretical and practical courses. These include statistics, mathematics, computer programming, information systems, project management, statistical process control, welding, and so on. In most cases, the community college will be happy to work with a local company in developing complementary training programs. In this way, the company gets the benefit of a larger training department than it actually operates.

Assurance of Qualification

The first reason for ensuring that only qualified people perform a job is obvious: it is to ensure quality of performance. In some cases, such as welding, nursing, or radiology, there may be a legal requirement. Whether legally required or not, the customer demands the best, which cannot be delivered consistently except by a trained, motivated workforce. One of the ways that employees are motivated is the second reason for ensuring that only qualified people perform a job: understanding that their training and skills are recognized by the company such that no lesser-trained person may perform their job. Their training gives them status.

Maintenance of Training Records

Again, there may be legal requirements to maintain training records, such as that required of airline pilots. This, however, should not be the main reason for records. We want to keep training records on our employees in order to identify their training progression. This progression has two purposes: the first to associate their skill with developments in the field, and the second to provide a base for career enhancement. We might think of it as depth and breadth of education and training. The training trail reveals not only what the employees can do, but what their potential is. Both the employees and their supervisor are responsible for maintaining the records, as well as for the training progression itself. Periodically, employee and supervisor review status, direction, and pace of the individual's training program.

Congruence

In Figure 4–3 we showed the fundamental units of *any* system, and one of these units is called the integrating function. We stress again that integration will not happen unless there is such a function in the system structure *at every point where integration is required.* The integrating function can be a physical mechanism or it can be a procedure systematically applied. Integration begins by identifying its need. What elements need to be brought together? Why? What will ensure their congruence? Large systems involve many persons and equipments over a widespread area. Generally, the work spaces are not mutually observable, one from the other. Even when they are, integration is not assured.

One day I became interested in observing an air operation aboard an aircraft carrier. Airplanes were to make threatening runs upon the ship, and the missile systems were to engage them in simulated defense. I approached the Project Supervisor, who was not in the Combat Information Center (CIC), but was in his stateroom reading a paperback. He informed me that the exercise was ongoing and did not require his presence. Upon entering CIC, I found that the air controller had put the aircraft in circular runs for want of knowing what else to do with them. The missile system trackers were at their consoles reading magazines. The Operations Officer, satisfied that his watch was clean, was preoccupied with some minor administrative business. No one knows where the Missile Officer was. Yet, the operation was on the ship's schedule. So much for integration. It doesn't happen unless we make it happen.

Can this happen in the private sector? How often have you walked into an office or shop and had to wait an interminable period of time before being waited on? How many universities have their professors moving in one direction and their students in another? These are examples of systems containing nonintegrated human components, but even manufactured systems, designed and built to be integrated *within their purview,* may not be fully integrated. We frequently purchase what turns out to be subsystems and must integrate them compatibly. At home, we have to integrate sound systems and computer input–output units made by different vendors. Generally, our manufacturing subprocesses also may be nonintegrated, and with unproven compatibility.

Process experts should establish the goals and objectives of the processes within their purview, as well as material and maintenance requirements. They will identify the input–output interface requirements of each process and arrange their arrival and departure in time and place as efficiently as possible according to the upstream and downstream systems. Where human activity is involved, procedures will be specified in detail, with appropriate cycle times and record keeping to verify procedural adherence. In this way the process becomes systematic, and quality shortcomings can be identified.

Effective integration requires process expertise from all the integrands and from the receptor processes. The objective is to achieve optimum timing and minimum loading of the interfaces. Loading mismatch causes excessive in-process inventory, over-burdened employees, and under- or overutilized equipment, at least, to say nothing of quality deterioration. The good news is that empowered employees will take it upon themselves to integrate their processes.

N O T E

1. **Systems Engineering.** There is little national agreement on what systems engineering is. Many people in industry have never heard of it. The term means one thing in the computer world, something else in the defense industry, and nothing at all to many companies and universities. As recently as 1991, only about a half dozen universities treated systems engineering as a distinct discipline. Most engineering schools continue to teach the traditional three: civil, mechanical, and electrical engineering. The problem with this tradition is that it does not fit into the modern era. These terms have little meaning on the large scale because there is no such thing as a large electronic system, for example. At some point, a large electronic

system crosses disciplines and involves mechanical and civil devices and analyses also. Thus, a wide variety of engineering expertise must be called in to design a large system, which typically contains embedded computers, moving mechanisms, large area distribution, and electronic control. From this point of view, systems engineering is that set of methodologies required to integrate the many system components. This may be quite a different approach from the traditional ones.

In order to attack the design of large systems, all the processes must be put in a mathematical form. Having done this, we are free of material constraints for the moment, and recognize immediately that the math model could just as well be a social, financial, or political system. However, such systems suggest operations research (OR). For this reason, there is an increasing association of systems engineering with OR and with industrial engineering. The University of Virginia has raised systems engineering to department level, and defines it as operations research plus policy analysis. I regret this because, although true enough, the definition excludes systems defined by the traditional engineering fields, with the result that more and more students without engineering educations gravitate to graduate systems engineering schools, and more and more traditional engineering schools look with disdain at systems engineering. These trends seriously limit the potential for systems engineering as a recognized discipline and especially as a career.

REFERENCES

Brecka, Jon, and Laura Rubach. "Corporate Quality Training Facilities." *Quality Progress,* January 1995, pp. 27–30.

Christison, William L. "Financial Information Is Key to Empowerment." *Quality Progress,* July 1994, pp. 47–48.

Drucker, Peter F. *The Frontiers of Management.* New York: Truman Talley Books, 1986.

Gibson, John E. *How to Do System Analysis.* Englewood Cliffs, NJ: Prentice Hall (in review).

Hersey, P., and K. Blanchard. *Management of Organizational Behavior.* Englewood Cliffs, NJ: Prentice Hall, 1982. © Center for Leadership Studies, Escondido, CA.

Kinlaw, Dennis C. *Continuous Improvement and Measurement for Total Quality.* San Diego, CA: Pfeiffer & Company, 1992.

Kinni, Theodore B. "The Empowered Workforce." Reprinted with permission from *Industry Week,* September 19, 1994. Copyright, Penton Publishing Inc., Cleveland, OH. Pp. 37–40.

Lamprecht, James L. *Implementing the ISO 9000 Series.* New York: Marcel Dekker, Inc., 1993. Reprinted by courtesy of Marcel Dekker, Inc.

Lapin, Lawrence L. *Quantitative Methods for Business Decisions.* New York: Harcourt Brace Jovanovich Inc., 1981.

Lowenthal, Jeffrey N. *Reengineering the Organization: A Step-by-Step Approach to Corporate Revitalization.* Milwaukee, WI: ASQC Quality Press, 1994.

MacKenzie, Kenneth D. *Organizational Design: The Organizational Audit and Analysis Technology.* Norwood, NJ: Ablex Publishing Corp., 1986.

Simmerman, Scott J. "The Square Wheels of Organizational Development." *Quality Progress,* October 1994, pp. 87–89.

Toelle, Richard A. "From 'Managing the Critical Path' to 'Managing Critical Activities.'" *Project Management Journal* 21 (December 1990), pp. 33–36.

Tomasko, Robert M. *Rethinking the Corporation.* New York: Copyright © 1993. Reprinted with permission of the publisher, AMACOM, a division of the American Management Association.

12

⑥ CONCLUSIONS

THE TASK AT HAND

All this will not be finished in the first 100 days. Nor will it be finished in the first 1,000 days, nor in the life of this Administration, nor even perhaps in our lifetime on this planet. But let us begin.

John F. Kennedy, Inaugural Address, 20 January 1961

Within the construct of constitutional government, the nature of the presidency is not significantly different from that of a CEO faced with reengineering his company. He has a view, a mission, and an agenda, but needs the agreement, wisdom, expertise, support, and cooperation of his peers, management, and personnel, as well as their good will. The task at hand is the same—to build a structure that can achieve the mission and goals of the company while withstanding the tests of time. As we have seen in the chapters of this book, there is much to do. It will take a long time. Let us begin.

We begin by thinking about what we want to do and where we want to go. We understand that there is a natural inhibition in thinking about novel ideas, and that boldness is required in order to explore the full dimension of our thoughts. We assign a mission for ourselves that embraces our goals and destiny, then determine policies that will get us there. We understand that a core ideology is necessary but not sufficient to build a quality company. We also need to integrate this philosophy into the fabric of the organization: goals, strategies, tactics, policies, processes, cultural practices, management behaviors, building layouts, pay systems, accounting systems, job design—everything the company does. The thinking, the results of the thinking, and the integration are *we* processes, where "we" is not an editorial pronoun but represents the people in the company. Reengineering is not a one-man show because business is a social activity and the best ideas are derived from the wisdom of the group.

The integrity of the company is achieved with a corporate structure, but its foundation is a company philosophy, which we have defined in the following way: *A set of guiding principles, driving forces, and ingrained attitudes that help communicate quality goals, plans, and policies to all employees and that are reinforced through conscious and subconscious behavior at all levels of the organization.*

ROBUST STRUCTURES REVIEWED

The structure we want to build must be robust, that is, it must be able to converge to an objective. This is possible only if all processes can converge to and maintain target values, behaviors, or objectives, irrespective of disturbances. Moreover, for improvability this property of convergence must be maintained even when target values change. This is so because as environmental conditions or customer requirements change, these changes must be anticipated or responded to with appropriate changes of our own in our objectives. The robust process translates the changed objectives to new decisions, actions, and target values.

Planning a robust structure precedes its building, and we plan dynamically. Dynamic quality planning establishes a time horizon, which includes not only the activity but time to observe results; a hierarchy of goals that lead from the tactical to strategic objectives; an organizational hierarchy that is fully integrated horizontally as well as vertically; a formal methodology that ensures systematic operation and process stability; a multiple-criteria decision system adapted to uncertain outcomes; and a control system for data collection and analysis, metrics for measurement of progress, and feedback for tracking and improvement.

The planning process will include interlevel committees to formulate ideas, policies, goals, and methods. The policies will be developed into action statements aimed at achieving the corporate mission. The goals will become the desired, measurable results of policy actions, and will be deployed with associated resources, responsibilities, integration, and "ownerships" for their achievement. Provision will be made for performance evaluation systems that identify what is to be evaluated, the metric, the methodology, and feedback for control and improvement.

The design of company processes will ensure that each process must have the attributes of stability, capability, and improvability, and have the three controls of responsibility, authority, and accountability. Design is based upon a simple assessment of verification and validation:

"Are we doing things right?"

"Are we doing the right things?"

Using the techniques discussed in Chapters 4 and 5, we design a robust process that will maintain the target value of a designated quality characteristic irrespective of perturbations. The same mechanism that provides convergence of the process to a target value also provides convergence to *any* desired value within the capability of the system, so that improvement is possible simply by selecting a new objective. We begin robust design by determining what our goal is, and designing a process to achieve that goal. Once the design is determined, we are ready to examine the dynamics of the designed process with an eye to stability. This is done by defining a system state and building a model with which we can identify stable properties. Having defined state variables, we are then ready to incorporate a convergence mechanism into the model and begin an optimization program that will determine those parameters that establish the most capable process. Then stability and capability parameters are built into a prototype process for on-line verification.

Of course, the heart of robustness is the ability to *control* the dynamics of a process. Every process must be closed. This means that every subprocess must be closed, because the difference between process, subprocess, and element of a process is simply perspective. Imagine that we can see the company as through a microscope with discrete power settings. At each level of magnification, we can view another level of aggregation and see a closed-loop system. This hierarchy of closed-loop control is needed to ensure robustness at all levels of operation.

With our processes designed, built, and functioning, we need to continually measure their stability, capability, and improvability. The measurements may be conducted by technical personnel, but the measurement system is enabled by management. Why? Because measurement is not a value-added process and is therefore subject to scrimping. This is the wrong view, but unfortunately, all too frequent. In a robust organization, managers need to measure performance for two very important reasons: to evaluate performance relative to goals, and to be able to control the process. And if Lord Kelvin is correct, then without measurement, we simply don't know what we're talking about.

We emphasize that robustness requires control, and control requires measurement. Substantive things can and must be measured, often objectively, perhaps subjectively. In keeping with Lord Kelvin, we know about them only to the extent that we measure them. Measurement is a discipline in itself, requiring knowledge about metrology and statistics as well as about the processes being measured. Even more than that, effective measurement of dynamic organizations requires a program of goals, policies, and procedures.

Management at the highest level needs to support the measurement of its processes. And when those responsible get to do the measuring, rather than "outsiders," they are encouraged to use the methods for improvement. The role of quality assurance in the matter is that of ensuring validity of application through joint meetings of process managers, supervisors, and workers, in which the details of theory and practice are worked out. It is important to include the workers because the charted process is often not the actual one. I know of production lines with ad hoc inspection points, a feature that has important statistical interpretation. The method must match the process, and that can be done through group agreement.

A system, its inputs, and its environment are all dynamic and interactive. Change in quality can come about through any or all of these media. The system can drift off its optimum settings, creating variation in state and output. The customer or supplier's needs may change, representing a variation in input. The operational environment may be modified by some new rule or intervention. These changes represent a disturbance to the status quo whether their effect is deliberate and benign, or inadvertent and adverse. For example, the disturbance may be applied deliberately, perhaps a decrease in personnel. It may be undesirable, as a power failure. Whatever its nature, a disturbance forces a change in system state and we want the system to respond to the change in a desirable way. Therefore, we design a corrective action capability to our processes to ensure desirable response of the system to change.

Corrective processes are a necessary but not sufficient complement of robust systems. They are necessary because they supply the mechanisms for convergence to target value. They are not sufficient because the target value of original design is a constant, whereas dynamic improvement implies a moving target. The essence of dynamic improvement is knowledge. The more we know about an environment or an input range, the better our predictive and deductive abilities. The timely use of knowledge for continual improvement of process is at the heart of an improvement program. This knowledge must be appropriately implemented and integrated into the corporate process structure. We make the subtle transition from corrective to robust systems by acquiring and applying knowledge appropriately, by exploiting the concepts of range and reach of process structure, and by accomplishing total system integration of all processes. We recognize that corrective and improvement processes are quite similar, the former looking back to see what doesn't track the existing objectives, the latter looking forward to new and presumably better objectives. Robustness is the result.

The key to it all is closed-loop control and total integration. The reengineering of a company is achieved in a transition along a time line that may be portrayed as a series of phases as shown in Figure 12–1. The figure is deliberately ambiguous, at first appearing as a fixed, closed-loop structure. In fact, it represents a transition in time from the inception of a mission statement to the culmination of a robust company. There is always customer interface, in keeping with the concept of quality management, and

FIGURE 12–1

The Phases of Transition to Robust Processes

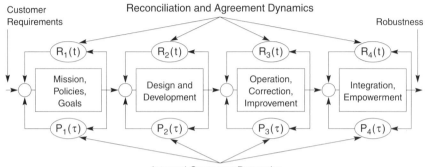

CUSTOMER EXPECTATIONS

there is always the driving force of the internal customer, in keeping with empowerment. But the internal customer concept is the first facet of empowerment and perhaps the most easy to initiate. It should begin right away, because without it, our processes won't operate acceptably. Without the internal customer, there is little responsibility or ownership, and without ownership we haven't begun integration.

The phases of Figure 12–1 are fairly obvious. We know them when we get there because we can measure their accomplishment. The external customer dynamics are represented by the symbol $R(t)$, implying a variable time dynamic that depends to a great extent upon the customer. The internal customer dynamics are represented by the symbol $P(\tau)$, implying the time constant of the phase, and depends upon company variables, parameters, and objectives. Management must recognize when the phase is achieved and when it is time to go on to the next phase.

The most difficult of all process dynamics is the integration, because it requires the willful cooperation of people. This is why empowerment is so important, albeit a very judicious transformation. If we think about it, we recognize that many of the initiatives of total quality management fall under the heading of empowerment, and can help to guide us in its establishment.

When empowerment is fully established, maximum integration is possible, robustness is in place, and company operations are on auto pilot. All processes are functioning in control, environmental and customer perturbations are anticipated or detected, and appropriate adaptations are made in policies, goals, and processes. Management and labor talk to each other, because each is fully invested in the other. Robustness.

AUTHOR INDEX

S U B J E C T   I N D E X